Moggies

A Book for Owners of Non-Pedigree Cats

Marianne Mays

Cover photo: Alan Robinson

foreword

Why write a book about non-pedigree cats? Well, if you consider that in most countries 80–90% of all cats are non-pedigrees (often referred to as 'moggies'), there's your answer! Hundreds of books are written about specific pedigree breeds, and most general cat books include large sections on pedigree cats. This book is intended as a sort of 'breed' book, but about non-pedigrees. After all, the great majority of cat owners will want information primarily about 'ordinary' cats, and there is much to be said for 'plain old moggies'. Before you take on that cute kitten from your neighbour's litter or adopt a cat or kitten from an animal shelter you will need to know something about general care, diet, how colour relates to temperament and various other topics. As well as dealing with these points, this book will tell you about all the fun you can have exhibiting your cat at cat shows. Yes, non-pedigree cats can be shown and win prizes, just like their pedigree counterparts. Showing cats can be a fulfilling hobby, whatever breed or type you keep and, assuming that you have gone about it in the correct way, your cat will enjoy it too.

Having said this, I must explain that I have nothing against pedigree cats. I have always found it very sad to hear people explain that they keep 'only pedigrees' or 'only moggies': a cat is a cat and will make a wonderful pet and companion whatever its appearance. My own home is shared with 20 cats; 17 of them pedigrees of three different breeds (Persians, Exotics and Siamese) and three of them 'ordinary' cats – although there isn't really anything ordinary about them. Like most cat breeders and exhibitors, I started off with one non-pedigree, and I would never be without at least one.

My very first cat was a non-pedigree Tabby called Felix who is still alive at the age of 17, living with my mother in Sweden. My elder daughter acquired her first cat at the tender age of six months, and that was a moggy, too. My husband also started off with a non-pedigree. Most moggies are rescued cats that have previously been abandoned, mistreated or simply unwanted. To highlight what excellent pets these unfortunate cats can make, and how rewarding it can be to give a home to a cat in need, this book also includes some stories about specific moggies, owned by my family and by other people. Real Cinderella stories they are as well! Read them and you will be amazed at how cruel some people can be, and at the incredible stamina of these cats. Then you will realise that there is nothing plain about the 'plain old moggy'.

Many thanks to all those people who have helped with this book:

- to everyone who sent me information about their own marvellous cats and photographs of them;
- to the British and American Cat Clubs for information on show rules;
- to the Governing Council of the Cat Fancy for allowing me to reproduce their show rules;
- to my husband Nick for writing the Cat History section and helping in many other ways;
- to my excellent vet, Chris Robinson, for posing for photographs and for invaluable health input;
- to Dale Briggs, owner of the *Paws for Thought* cat emporium in Leeds, for letting us photograph some of his stock of feline equipment;
- to Mr and Mrs Hussey, owners of *Animal Fayre Pet Store* in Havant, Hants, who also allowed us to photograph their stock;
- and to anyone else who helped out in one way or another.

I simply couldn't have written this book without you all.

Many thanks.

Marianne Mays

This book is dedicated to all my non-pedigree cats, past and present: Felix, Tippi, Hamish, Benji, Silky, Pansy and Felicia. Without them this book would never have been written.

chapter
one
introduction

WHAT IS A NON-PEDIGREE CAT?

The non-pedigree cat is known by many different names, such as moggy, mog, household pet, household cat and ordinary domestic cat. Whatever you prefer to call it, for the purpose of this book a non-pedigree cat is defined as a cat of mixed breeding: either the common 'moggy' in which no particular breed characteristic can be seen or the cross-breed, where it may be obvious that one parent was of a specific breed, such as Siamese. Technically speaking, a pure-bred cat without its pedigree papers could also be defined as a 'non-pedigree' because of the lack of documentation, but this book will deal only with those cats that are either of no particular breed at all or cross-breeds.

BRIEF HISTORY OF THE DOMESTIC CAT

The origins of the domestic cat are a subject for conjecture. There are about 25 species of small wild cat throughout the world, many of which can interbreed, producing hybrid species.

There are three likely contenders for the 'official' ancestry of today's domestic cat:

- African Wild Cat *(Felis libyca)*.

- Forest Wild Cat *(Felis silvestris)*, closely related to the African Wild Cat, ranging across mainland Europe and Britain.

- Jungle Cat *(Felis chaus)*, known to be domesticated by the Ancient Egyptians as far back as 2000 BC.

Over the centuries, Man would have bred domesticated versions of all these species and eventually, no doubt, interbred them, leading to today's domestic cat, *Felis cattus*.

GODS AND DEVILS

Domestic cats have had a chequered history as far as their association with Man goes, which says more about the fickle, superstitious nature of *Homo sapiens* than about the Feline species.

The Ancient Egyptians were the first civilised culture to domesticate the cat. Originally, cats were probably domesticated for the practical purpose of killing vermin such as rats and mice in the city granaries. Paintings dating back as far as 2000 BC show cats (undoubtedly trained jungle cats). These seem to have been trained as 'retriever' cats (a rôle more often associated with dogs) and are shown accompanying Egyptian men on hunting expeditions. However, there are no written records of Egyptian 'hunting cats' and current thought tends towards the theory that such Cat and Man hunting scenes are allegorical, possibly religious, in context rather than factual. We shall probably never know.

In later times, cats became revered as gods, or reincarnations of priests. One of the Egyptians' most revered deities was Bastet or Bast, a goddess with the head of a cat and the body of a woman. Bast was the goddess of fertility and a huge and popular cult grew up around her, including festivals at which there was much merry-making and - not surprisingly for a fertility goddess - much love-making. No wonder the 'Cult of the Cat' was so popular with the Egyptians.

So cats became pampered, revered and treated to the very best of domesticated life by the Ancient Egyptians. When they died, the cats were embalmed and mummified, just like important human beings such as the Pharaohs. Today, many of these ancient cat mummies can be seen in museums around the world. After the Roman Legions conquered Cleopatra's Egypt in 30 BC the domesticated cat spread further throughout the world. Many were taken from Egypt by Roman legionnaires. The cat was still considered to be lucky, although it was never revered as a god again.

The cat's fortunes changed for the worse in the Middle Ages, when the Christian Church began its horrific campaign against witchcraft. Those accused of being witches were nearly always women. Cats were perceived to be agents of the devil and persecuted with as much hatred and vigour as people accused of being witches. The usual scenario was for an old woman living alone with just a pet cat for company to be denounced as a witch and arrested. She would then be tortured into confessing that she was a witch, whereupon she would be burnt at the stake or drowned. Cats were cruelly persecuted without any pretence at a trial. The Church said they were agents of the devil or indeed devils in feline form. Sackfuls of cats were burnt on bonfires, to the delight of the masses. Others were drowned, hanged or thrown from high buildings. Europe in the Middle Ages was not a good place to be a cat.

Eventually, the witch hunting died down and cats were left alone. Their old rôle as vermin-killers in granaries and barns was appreciated, and this was where they remained until the eighteenth century, when some more affluent and intelligent people began to keep cats as pets in their houses again. There was no divine worship this time, but the status of many domestic cats improved greatly.

THE CAT FANCY

From their acceptance as domestic pets it was only a relatively short time until cats were seen as desirable show animals, and this led to the formation of the organised Cat Fancy. The very first cat show was staged by cat-lover Harrison Weir in 1871. The growth of the Cat Fancy led to the diversification of different 'fancy' breeds of cat. This in turn led to a greater public demand for pet cats from people of all classes.

Today, domestic cats are extremely popular pets. In 1995 a detailed survey in Great Britain revealed that, for the first time, cats were numerically more popular as pets than dogs. Although the many different breeds of pedigree cat have varying degrees of popularity, the ordinary, common-or-garden moggy remains far and away the most popular pet domestic cat.

ADVANTAGES AND DISADVANTAGES OF NON-PEDIGREE VERSUS PEDIGREE CATS

Why do some people choose to keep only non-pedigrees, others pedigrees only, and yet others, such as myself, both? Ask 10 different people and you will probably get 10 different answers. Some may say that moggies are healthier than pedigree cats and have better temperaments. Others may say that a pedigree is very much a known quantity, as you can find out before the actual purchase all the necessary details about such topics as behaviour and longevity. I would say cats are cats, and they are all individuals. True, you may get two Persians, or two non-pedigree tabbies, that share the same behavioural patterns, but you will hardly ever meet two cats that share exactly the same characteristics, health and stamina. Whatever your choice, you can never be quite sure how that particular cat will turn out.

A clear advantage of the non-pedigree is that it is generally very long-lived and healthy, seldom succumbing to disease. The average moggy will probably live between 15 and 20 years and, if looked after properly (which includes receiving preventative medical treatment such as annual booster inoculations), will seldom fall ill. I have noticed that my moggies seem to have 'stomachs made of steel', and whenever my pedigree cats suffer from stomach upsets (perhaps after a change of food) the others are all right. On the other hand, unlike the pedigrees, they are not usually happy to be kept indoors all the time, so are more likely to be victims of road accidents or dog attacks. They are also far more likely than indoor pedigree cats to catch any of the serious feline diseases, such as Feline Leukaemia or Feline Immunodeficiency Virus, as these are primarily spread through fighting between outdoor cats.

As far as temperament is concerned, you will nearly always know something of how a pedigree cat will behave, even if the behaviour varies slightly between individuals. For instance, most Persians will be laid back 'lap cats' that happily spend all their time in front of the fire, and most Siamese will be highly intelligent, lively and vocal. With a non-pedigree, temperament is pot luck. It can be said to a certain degree that temperament is usually the same within one particular colour of moggy (more about this in Chapter 2). However, with the non-pedigree you are far more likely to start out with a friendly and playful kitten that grows up to be a solitary and fairly grumpy cat. If you need to make absolutely sure that the kitten you choose will grow up to be good-natured (for example, if you have young children) you will be better off choosing a pedigree breed known to have a placid temperament. But that is not to deny that many non-pedigrees will grow up to be marvellous pets for young and old alike. It is simply that, with a moggy, you never really know - which, of course, is part of their charm.

Cat naps are necessary for all felines, lions and fire-side moggies alike.

As far as price is concerned, a non-pedigree is not likely to be expensive. You can probably find kittens advertised as 'free to good homes', or adopt one for a small sum from a local animal shelter. But remember that your non-pedigree will still need to be vaccinated, neutered and wormed. A pedigree cat bought for several hundred pounds may seem expensive, but will invariably be fully vaccinated and free of worms, fleas and the other unpleasant parasites with which many moggies arrive in their new homes. A pedigree cat will also have been bred carefully from disease-free parents who have been blood-tested to make sure that they are perfectly healthy, whereas a non-pedigree will probably be the result of an unplanned mating, and so may or may not carry disease. Money should not therefore be a consideration when you make your choice, as the moggy is likely to need more veterinary care initially. After all, all cats eat the same amount of food, need the same annual injections and cost as much to neuter.

So, there you have it. No cat is entirely without its good or bad points. Do bear in mind the various considerations that I have mentioned, even if you end up simply choosing the cat or kitten that appeals the most to you, for whatever reason. Kittens are always irresistible, whether pedigree or not, and there will probably be one that you will fall for the moment that you set eyes on it - even if it is the opposite of what you had planned to get.

chapter two

acquiring a non-pedigree cat

WHERE TO FIND A NON-PEDIGREE CAT

Once you have decided that you do want a non-pedigree, your next question will be where to find a suitable cat or kitten. There is never a shortage of non-pedigree cats looking for good homes. Unfortunately, there are far more in need of homes than there are good homes available. Every year animal sanctuaries are having to put thousands of cats to sleep simply because there are too many of them. The one you acquire will almost certainly be unwanted or rescued, so you will be giving the cat the gift of life simply by giving it a home. There are many different ways of acquiring non-pedigree cats, but I will list the most common ones here.

THE ANIMAL SHELTER

There are hundreds of animal shelters in most countries. In England, the best known one is the RSPCA, a national charity that has regional animal homes all over the country. There are many others, some run by national charities, others by local ones. You will find details of these in your local telephone directory, and your veterinary surgeon should also be able to point you in the right direction.

An animal shelter is an excellent place to visit when you want to acquire a non-pedigree cat or kitten. All the cats there will have been rescued for one reason or another; they may have been abandoned and picked up as strays, handed in to the shelter by the previous owner for some reason, or taken away from an uncaring owner. All cats in such a place will have had some veterinary attention to ensure that they are healthy, and none will be re-homed unless it is fit enough. The staff at the shelter will be able to tell you the cat's background as well as its general behaviour and temperament, and they may be able to advise you which cat to choose to suit your particular wishes and circumstances. On the other hand, the staff at the shelter will not let you adopt a cat unless they are convinced that you will look after it properly. You will probably be asked to fill in a question-naire answering such questions as where you live, whether you have any children or pets, and whether you have owned a cat previously. You will be asked to sign a form, undertaking to care for the cat and to have it neutered unless this has already been done. At some shelters you may be asked for references from people who have already adopted an animal from there, or the staff may wish to make a home visit so that they can make sure that your home is suitable for a cat. None of this should put you off; it is all in the best interests of the cat and, if you are a genuine, caring cat-lover, you will have nothing to hide. Most animal shelters make a charge for cats or ask for a donation. This is partly to discourage people from acquiring a cat simply because it is free, and partly to recover some of the costs which have been incurred, such as for food and veterinary care. As part of the adoption process, many shelters offer vouchers which partly or completely cover the cost of having your cat neutered, and this is an excellent idea. Most vets accept these vouchers.

A rescue centre is an excellent place from which to buy your non-pedigree cat.

Semi-longhaired white rescued cat Tanya with owners Pat Creaton and Carol Walker of the South Ribble Pet Cat Club.

CAT RESCUE ORGANISATIONS

These are similar to animal shelters, but cat rescue organisations deal with cats only. The large national organisations such as the Cats' Protection League have regional catteries that you can visit. Smaller organisations may not have catteries; instead they have a network of foster homes. The fosterers are members of the organisation who have agreed to care for rescued cats until suitable homes can be found. The same rules apply as for the animal shelter. Organisations like these may not be listed in the telephone directory, but they often advertise in local newspapers; your vet will have details.

CAT CLUBS

Many cat clubs have rescue sections, again often operating by means of foster homes. Breed clubs may cater only for their particular breed, but general cat clubs may well rescue and re-home non-pedigrees as well. There are also special cat clubs for ordinary domestic pets, such as the West Riding Pet Cat Club in Yorkshire in England, and these do excellent work in rescuing and re-homing cats. You may find details of these clubs in the various cat magazines and they often put advertisements in pet shop windows and at veterinary surgeries. Again, strict rules apply for anybody wishing to adopt a cat from a cat club rescue centre.

ADVERTISEMENTS

Non-pedigree kittens from unplanned litters (which means nearly all of them) will often be advertised, either for sale or as free to good homes. You will find advertisements like this in your local newspapers, in pet shop windows, on notice boards and sometimes your local vet will know of kittens looking for homes. Many cat owners acquired their first cat in this fashion. I did myself. My first moggy, a Tabby called Felix, was bought through an advertisement in a newspaper. Such kittens are nearly always in great need of good homes, being the results of accidental matings and therefore unwanted. Many uncaring owners of such kittens will consider destroying them, often by drowning, if homes cannot be found quickly enough. So do not feel that you are doing the kitten less of a favour by buying it from somebody who advertised kittens for sale rather than from a shelter. However, **never** buy a kitten from somebody who deliberately breeds from his or her non-pedigrees. With so many unwanted kittens around, deliberate breeding of non-pedigrees should never occur, and anybody trying to cash in on people wanting such a kitten should be avoided. After all, if you buy a kitten, this person will only be encouraged to breed another litter.

One problem with buying a kitten from somebody advertising is that it can be difficult to know what you are letting yourself in for. Unlike the caring pedigree breeder, the breeder of these kittens will not have made sure that the parents were healthy, so the kittens may carry disease. Unlike those from a shelter or cat club, the kittens will not have been examined by a vet before adoption takes place, so you are likely to end up with a kitten that has parasites such as fleas, worms and ear mites, and that has not been vaccinated. As most owners of unwanted kittens simply want to get rid of them as quickly as possible, nearly all will be sold too young, before they have been properly weaned. It is important to have any such kitten examined by a vet at the first opportunity so that you can get proper advice on such points as feeding, worming and vaccinations. Never assume that a kitten is healthy simply because it looks all right; always let your vet check the kitten over.

Good companions: two cats will keep each other company.

PET SHOPS

Not many pet shops sell kittens these days, but some still do so. The kittens in a pet shop may have been unwanted ones taken in by the pet shop owner, or they may have been bred specifically for sale by him or her. They are usually non-pedigrees.

Whether you buy a kitten from a pet shop should depend on the shop itself. A good, caring pet shop that has taken in an unwanted litter of kittens may be as good a place as any from which to acquire an ordinary kitten. Such a shop should house the kittens in large pens comfortably furnished with beds, litter trays, food and water bowls and toys, and the kittens should not be where customers can disturb them all day long. After all, like any babies, kittens need plenty of sleep. Ideally, these kittens should be let out of their pen for some exercise a few times every day (when there are no customers in the shop). The pet shop staff should be able to give you correct advice on feeding, vaccinations and general care of a kitten and should not sell you a kitten unless they have made reasonably sure that you will give it a good home.

Unfortunately, not all shops that deal in kittens are like this, and those that are less than caring should be avoided. If you buy a kitten from a pet shop in which the staff do not take proper care of the kittens you will only encourage them to sell more. If everybody refused to buy kittens from such shops they would have no choice but to stop selling kittens.

Having said that, I know very well how difficult it can be to resist a little kitten in a pet shop, especially if it is obvious that the kitten is not being looked after properly. The urge to take it home is absolutely overwhelming. Two of my non-pedigrees were purchased from unscrupulous pet shops and I tend to classify them as 'rescued'.

Benji, a tabby-and-white male, was only six weeks old when he was offered for sale in a pet shop. He was far too young to be away from his mother, and looked very lost. On closer inspection, he was found to have fleas and worms. I bought him; the shop assistant was not even able to sex him and I was offered no advice whatsoever, nor were any questions asked. Benji was simply shoved into a small cardboard box, and money changed hands.

He cost me a small fortune in veterinary fees, and for the first couple of weeks I had to bottle-feed him with milk, as he obviously missed his mother. He had not yet lost the urge to suckle, although he was able to lap milk from a saucer and eat solid food. He even used to wake me up in the middle of the night, asking for his bottle. His favourite resting place was the top of my head, in the middle of my hair, presumably because this reminded him of his mother's fur. Today he is a large, tough and fairly grumpy cat who catches rats and mice regularly, but he has never quite lost that behaviour pattern from the first few weeks with me: even now he will snuggle up close to my hair, knead with his paws, purr and dribble, just like a small kitten. No kitten deserves to start life like this.

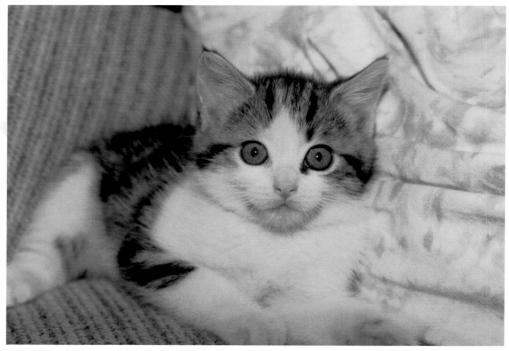

Benji was only six weeks old when we acquired him.

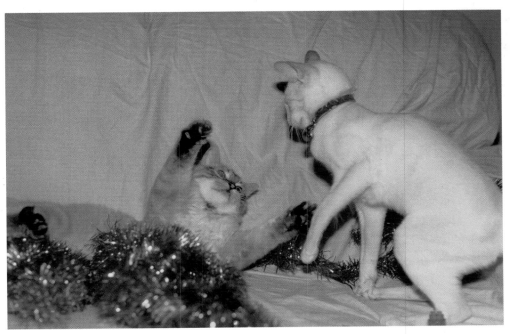

'Come on - let's play!'

The other cat, Pansy, was purchased from a different pet shop, but under very similar circumstances.

STRAYS

Many people acquire their first moggy by starting to feed a stray cat or kitten that eventually moves in and becomes a permanent member of the household. There is nothing wrong with this, and it can be marvellous to gain a cat's trust gradually. However, before you start to feed a cat or kitten that appears to be a stray, please do all you can to check that the cat really **is** a stray. Cats are opportunists and most are very greedy, thinking nothing of acting as a stray to gain an extra meal. If the cat is wearing no collar, ask around or advertise to find out whether it already has a home somewhere. If it has, do not feed it. If you find that you have given a home to a genuine stray, then once again it is important to take the cat along to your vet for a check-up, which should include vaccinations and neutering.

If you are known to be an animal lover you may very well find a couple of children on your doorstep one day, complete with kitten or cat, asking you to give it a home for one reason or another. Often the reason given is that the child's parents won't allow him or her to keep the cat and have threatened to have it put to sleep if a new home cannot be found. This is emotional blackmail, but what do you do? It has happened to me and my family several times, and we have never been able to say no. If you do take in the cat or kitten, you can either keep it after your vet has checked it over, or you can contact your local RSPCA or cat shelter, asking them to collect the cat; they will normally do so.

ADULT OR KITTEN

Whether you acquire a kitten or an adult will depend on your personal preference and circumstances. Most people will fall for a cute little kitten, but please do consider giving a home to an adult rescued cat. All rescue organisations find that kittens are far easier to re-home than adult cats, so it is usually the adults that have to be put to sleep because of lack of space. If your circumstances permit you to take on an adult cat it is well worth considering.

It is best if anyone wanting to give a home to an adult cat does not have any other fully-grown cats, as it can be extremely difficult, if not impossible, to introduce two adult cats to each other successfully. This is especially true if you already have a cat that you have kept for a few years. Your existing cat will be used to being a single cat and is not likely to tolerate an adult feline intruder in its home. A kitten, on the other hand, will usually be accepted, even if the adult is somewhat reluctant to start with. Similarly, if you have a dog, a kitten may be the better option, as you have no way of knowing how an adult cat will react to a dog. A kitten that is allowed to grow up with a well-behaved dog will probably always like dogs, but an adult may have had bad experiences in the past. Finally, if you have young children, do not take on an adult cat unless you are sure that the cat is good-tempered and will tolerate the presence of children. Ask at the rescue centre whether they can recommend any particular cat. Again, it is quite possible that an adult rescued cat may have had bad experiences with children in the past.

You should also make sure that your children are safe for cats, adults or kittens. All children need to be taught respect for animals and, whereas an obedient dog often will put up with teasing and harassment from children who have not been taught any better, a cat is likely to defend itself.

If you have no other pets and no children an adult cat could be ideal. You will find it very rewarding to give a home to a cat that may never have known comfort or kindness in all its life. An adult cat may be easier to cope with than an exuberant kitten, as it is far less likely to get up to such pranks as climbing the curtains and knocking over your potted plants. There are, of course, exceptions ...

MALE OR FEMALE

What sex you choose is again very much a matter of personal preference. Males and females make equally good pets, **provided that they are neutered**. Therefore, gender need not influence your choice of cat.

ONE OR TWO

Should you have one or two cats? The simple answer is: two. Cats love company, and a cat that has the companionship of other feline friends will generally be much happier than a single one. There is the added advantage that two cats will keep each other company if you go out to work all day, so you need not worry about them feeling lonely in your absence.

A single cat will probably become very devoted to you, its owner, as you will become a sort of substitute cat. But a cat that has been kept as sole feline for years probably will never accept the presence of another cat in the house. Personal expe-

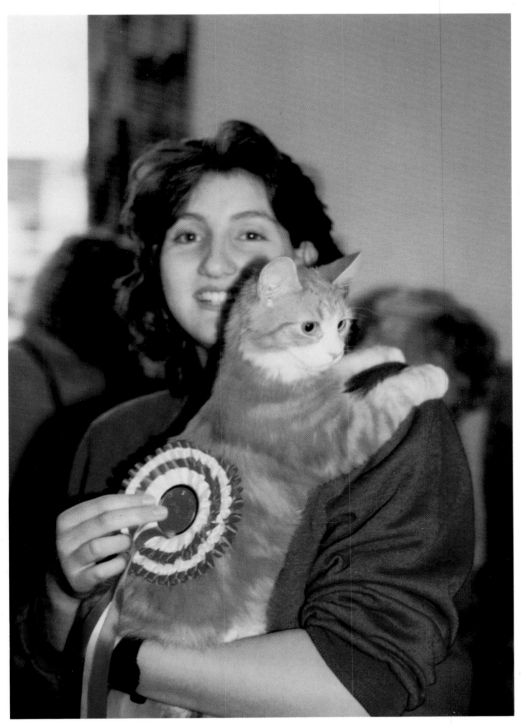

Rory the Red wins a red rosette.

Tippi the non-pedigree tabby with Siamese friend Tolly.

rience tells me that cats kept singly are far more likely to sleep most of the time and less likely to play; with age they often become slightly grumpy or bad-tempered. A cat that has feline companionship tends to be more active throughout its life, retaining some 'kittenish' characteristics such as playing with toys. Single cats often tend to turn into fairly boring creatures as they grow old, preferring to do nothing but eat and sleep. Anyone who has seen two cats (or even four or five) cuddled up or playing together will realise that this is what they really want. A cat that is one of a pair or a group does not necessarily make a worse pet than a single cat. It will be less dependent on you but it will still love to sit on your lap and have a good purr. We have 20 cats in this house, and every single one of them enjoys the company of both other cats and humans.

HOW TO CHOOSE

Many people will find that they never actually had a chance to choose their cat; it may simply have been a stray that decided to move in, or perhaps somebody turned up on your doorstep with it. If that is the case you will have to make the best of the situation. Take the cat to be checked over carefully by your vet as soon as possible. Never introduce an unknown cat to any existing cat before it has been to the vet; you can never know for certain whether it carries disease, even if it appears perfectly healthy. The vet will check it for any obvious signs of disease (a runny nose or eyes may indicate cat influenza) and for parasites such as fleas and ear mites, and will tell you how to go about worming it. Since a cat with an unknown past is unlikely to be vaccinated, it should be assumed not to be, and the vaccination should be carried out as soon as possible. One injection will be given to start with and another three weeks later. The cat will then need to receive one booster injection every 12 months to keep its immunity. Former strays are hardly ever neutered, and your vet will be able to tell you whether a male cat has been neutered. If it has not you should arrange for this to be done as soon as possible.

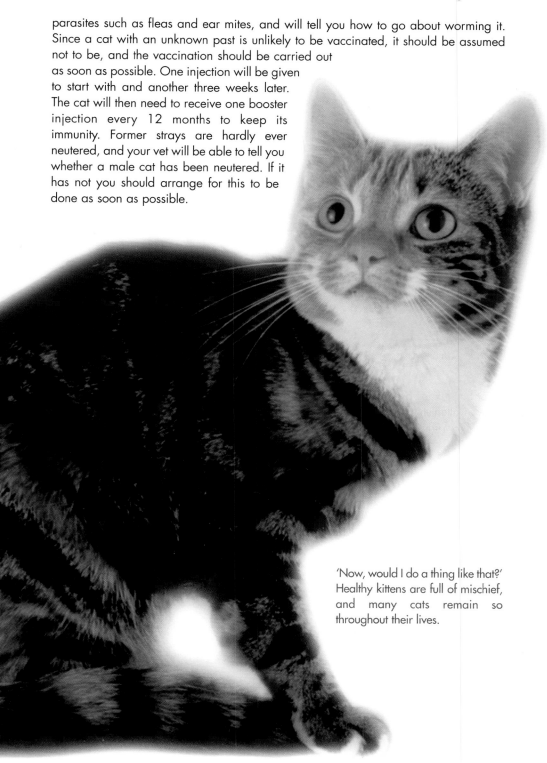

'Now, would I do a thing like that?' Healthy kittens are full of mischief, and many cats remain so throughout their lives.

In the case of a female it is often far more difficult to be able to tell. On some cats it may be possible to feel the rows of stitches put inside them after neutering (often referred to as 'spaying' for females), but this is not always possible. If there is any doubt, the only way is for your vet to examine your cat under general anaesthetic. If she has not been neutered, the vet will neuter her then and there; if she has, it is just a case of stitching her up again. She will be none the worse for the experience.

One very important factor to bear in mind when you acquire a rescued cat (and this means any cat that has not been bred by a *bona fide* cat breeder) is that you do not know whether it carries disease. Two fatal diseases are spread through biting and mating. Any cat that has been outdoors or has been bred from parents that are not certified free of these diseases may be infected. The two diseases are Feline Leukaemia Virus (FeLV) and Feline Immunodeficiency Virus (FIV). Both are incurable and ultimately fatal. However, an affected cat can have the disease for up to two years before symptoms start to show, so the fact that the cat **looks** healthy is no guarantee whatsoever.

The only way to know for sure whether your cat is infected is to have it blood-tested by your vet. All responsible breeders of pedigree cats do this as a matter of course before allowing any cat to be mated but, as most non-pedigrees are the results of accidental matings, hardly any have been tested. I cannot over-emphasise how **vital** it is to have your cat tested. After all, if the cat is positive for either FeLV or FIV it is a great health risk to other cats and must never be allowed out, or to mix with your other cats. Unfortunately, no vaccine is available as yet against FIV, but there is one against FeLV. Bear in mind, though, that it is pointless to vaccinate your cat against FeLV unless it has tested negative first; otherwise you may end up with a vaccinated cat that is still positive for the disease.

If you are lucky enough to be able to choose a cat or kitten, there are some simple rules that should be followed. If you acquire your cat from a rescue centre of any kind you can be fairly certain that the cat is a healthy one, as the centre will have had it checked over by a vet. However, you should still ask whether or not the cat has been tested for FeLV and FIV (not all rescues do), whether it has been vaccinated, and whether it has been neutered.

If you pick a kitten from a litter advertised in your local newspaper then, just as with a stray, you should take it to a vet for examination as soon as possible. When you choose your kitten, look it over carefully from head to tail. Are the ears clean? If a crusty, near-black discharge can be seen inside them the kitten probably has ear mites, so will need veterinary treatment. Are the eyes clear and dry? Is the nose dry? Runny eyes and nose may indicate cat influenza, so beware. Next check the fur. Is it clean? Signs of fleas will include small black specks of flea dirt. The presence of fleas is not a serious affliction in itself and can easily be eradicated with a good-quality flea spray, but fleas play a part in the reproductive cycle of the tapeworm, so a kitten with fleas is more likely to have worms. Still, any unwormed kitten should be wormed on arrival in its new home. Your vet will advise you on this.

Signs of worms will include a distended belly with a sharp, thin back and a dull coat. Occasionally worms can be seen in the cat's faeces and around its anus. (See Chapter 7: Healthcare.) Check that the skin appears clean and unbroken, as any spots, scratches or lesions may be a sign of ringworm, a fungus which is notoriously difficult to eradicate and which may affect humans and other animals as well as cats. Check that the cat's tail area is clean and dry; soiling of this area indicates diarrhoea.

Finally, check the kitten's behaviour. When it is fully awake, is it alert and interested in what is going on around it? A kitten that just keeps still in a corner is likely to be ill and a very shy kitten may well grow up to be a very shy adult. Healthy kittens are full of life and always up to mischief, taking great delight in meeting new people and hardly staying still for a moment. Except, that is, when they sleep, and kittens tend to sleep often. However, curiosity comes before sleep, and any normal kitten that is faced with a stranger will want to check this out before continuing its nap.

As far as temperament is concerned, it is very difficult to assess how a kitten will behave when it grows up. If it is at all possible, you should ask to meet the kitten's mother, as she will be your best guide. If she is friendly, then the likelihood is that her kittens will be. If, on the other hand, she is very shy and perhaps even hisses at you, then her kittens will probably be shy too.

A tabby-and-white cat, with friend, showing off its lovely 'shirt front'.

CHOOSING BY COLOUR

Believe it or not, one other way to try to ensure that you will have a friendly, laid-back adult cat is to choose the colour wisely. It may sound unlikely, but anyone who has been involved in non-pedigree cats for any length of time will tell you that certain behavioural patterns can be linked to colour. Given that temperament varies considerably between individuals, it may still be worth bearing the following notes on colour in mind when choosing a kitten.

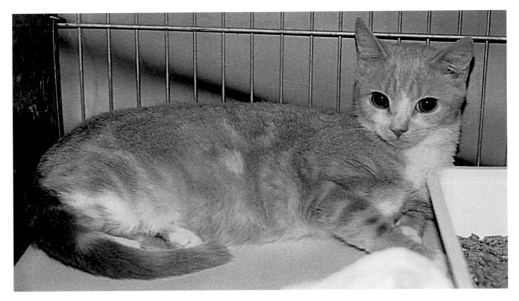

A cream-and-white kitten. Cream is not so common as ginger in non-pedigree cats.

Tabby

Your typical moggy is very often an ordinary brown tabby cat, with or without white markings. A tabby is the sort of cat that prefers to spend most of its time outdoors, rather than purring on its owner's lap. It will do this too, but only when **it** feels like it! Tabbies are excellent mousers and have been known to bring their owners all sorts of prey. Benji, my own tabby, brought me live goldfish, obviously stolen from some neighbour's pond, on two occasions. Tabbies are very independent, and therefore often object to being handled unless the invitation comes from them. Having said that, there are always exceptions. In 1994, at the Supreme Cat Show, Best In Show Non-pedigree was awarded to a tabby-and-white cat who obviously didn't mind being handled at all, even by several strangers. Tabby cats come in several different colours and markings, although most people tend to think of just one particular variety when referring to a tabby.

The 'ordinary' tabby cat that we so often see is a brown classic tabby, sometimes referred to as a 'blotched tabby'. The fur is a greyish brown (shades can vary) with black tabby markings. These include striped legs and tail, stripes on the face (an 'M' can usually be seen clearly on the forehead) and both stripes and patches on the body. The belly, unless white, is beige with black spots.

The second most common tabby is the striped or mackerel. This cat is coloured like the classic tabby, but has even, thin stripes all along its body, rather like a miniature tiger.

The spotted tabby is the rarest, not seen very often in non-pedigree cats. This cat has the same stripy legs and tail as the other tabbies, but its body is covered with even spots rather than stripes.

As far as colour is concerned, the most common tabby is the brown. Silver, red and blue tabbies are seen in non-pedigree cats, but far less frequently. Their behaviour patterns often correspond to their particular colour rather than to the fact that they are tabbies.

Black

The black cat is very strong-willed and independent and, unless the owner has spent a considerable amount of time getting to know his or her cat, is likely always to remain 'The Cat That Walks By Himself' (or in the company of other cats). Black cats can become fairly aggressive and may be very difficult to deal with. In fact, there may be a good reason why witches' cats are traditionally black! On the other hand, a black cat that has become truly devoted to its owner will be a wonderful pet, a companion not to be equalled. Again, the title Best In Show Non-pedigree at the Supreme Cat Show has been won by all-black cats.

Black-and-white

Black-and-white cats are generally far easier to deal with than those that are completely black and they usually make very good pets and companions.

Patchwork Pansy, a pretty tortie-and-white cat belonging to the author's daughter, Rebecca.
Photo: Alan Robinson

Ginger

Ginger cats are also very common. Sometimes referred to as 'marmalade', technically speaking these cats are red or red tabby. They are very popular as pets and non-pedigree show cats, as they are often very friendly and playful. However, as with many red-haired animals (including people) they can be quite fiery at times. Ginger cats are often seen with white markings.

People often say that all ginger cats are male, but this is not true. Most ginger cats are male because, if a ginger tom mates with, say, a black female, then all the male kittens will be ginger, and all the females will be tortoiseshell, a colour only seen in females. However, ginger females do exist, so never assume that a cat is male simply because it is ginger.

Tortoiseshell

Tortoiseshell cats make wonderful pets. They are friendly and outgoing and often remain playful well into adulthood, whereas many other cats tend to lose their kitten behaviour once they are out of kittenhood. Some of the most attractive cats to be seen are tortoiseshells. They are nearly always female, as the gene responsible for this particular colouring is a sex-linked one only passed to female kittens. Ginger toms are usually responsible for fathering tortoiseshell kittens, but cream toms also produce tortoiseshell, as do ginger or tortoiseshell queens. Very occasionally, a male tortoiseshell kitten will be born. This is essentially a 'freak of nature' and such cats are usually infertile. They will be perfectly healthy cats, however.

Tortoiseshells come in many different colours and can look very different from each other. Despite the fact that it is one of the most common colour combinations, you will seldom, if ever, see two identical 'torties'. There are two main types: tortoiseshell and tortoiseshell-and-white. A tortie cat without any white will have two colours that are evenly intermingled with each other, giving the effect of a 'marbled' cat. The effect will be very much the same if the cat has some slight white markings, such as white paws (but not legs) and a white chest. However, if the cat is tortie with a substantial amount of white, then the appearance is altogether different. Such cats will often have completely white legs and the entire chest and belly will be white, with a large amount of white on the face. Occasionally, you will get cats that are mainly white, with tortoiseshell patches. In both these cases, each patch will be large and clearly defined. The two non-white colours will be intermingled hardly at all, but will consist of large patches on the white, of roughly the same area.

The most common tortoiseshell colour is black and ginger (red), with or without white. Another combination seen frequently is blue and cream. Such a cat can be referred to as a 'blue tortie', a 'blue-cream' or a 'dilute tortie'. (The word 'dilute' refers to the fact that, if a tortoiseshell cat's black and red colours are diluted or 'bleached' by a natural genetic process, black becomes blue and red becomes cream.)

The third most common tortie is the tortie tabby, which is simply brown tabby with ginger mixed in. Among the rarer colours is the silver tabby tortie, which is silver tabby with cream. Other colours do exist, but non-pedigree tabbies of these colours are hardly ever seen.

Two feline stars of *Heartbeat:* Arnie and Hebe.

White

White cats are very pretty, but relatively uncommon. They can have either blue or orange eyes, or one eye of each colour, which is known as 'odd-eyed'. Some non-pedigree whites show a small patch of colouring (usually black) right on top of their heads.

Whites are usually nice, friendly cats. Unfortunately, white colouring is often linked to inherited deafness. This is especially true of blue-eyed white cats. In pedigree cats, breeders have tried very hard to eradicate this genetic problem but among non-pedigrees, which are bred by accident, it is a recurring problem. If the cat has one blue and one orange eye it may be deaf in the ear on the same side as the blue eye. So, if you intend to give a home to a white kitten, first check that its hearing is normal. This can be done by making noises, such as clapping your hands, near the kitten. Any normal kitten should respond immediately by either turning its head towards the source of the noise or twitching its ears. Deaf cats can make very nice pets and live happy lives but, needless to say, they will need special consideration. For instance, it would not be a good idea to let a deaf cat go out, as it would not be able to hear such dangers as oncoming traffic.

Blue

Blue cats are often referred to as 'smoky grey', and blue is really a diluted version of black. Therefore, a blue's temperament can be similar to a black's, although it may not be quite as strong-willed. Blue is not one of the more common colours among non-pedigrees.

Hubert (part Russian blue). This attractive non-pedigree cat belongs to Ann-Sofi Andersson of Sweden. Photo: Anders Mall

Others

Non-pedigree cats can come in any other colour: silver tabby, shaded silver, smoke, cream - the sky's the limit! However, most non-pedigree cats of these more exotic colours are the result of a mating of a pedigree cat with a moggy, or two pedigree cats of different breeds. For this reason, it can be difficult to predict their temperaments, although it is probably fair to say that any non-pedigree cat that is born from one pedigree parent will probably have a strong resemblance to that parent in both colour and temperament.

Longhairs

Non-pedigree longhairs are quite common. Generally, it can be said that any moggy with long fur is likely to be slightly more laid-back than its shorthaired counterpart.

SETTLING THE CAT INTO ITS NEW HOME

Whether it is a kitten or an adult, when you bring your new cat home it should be transported securely in a proper cat-carrier (see Chapter 2: General Care). Never accept a cardboard box or a cat-carrier made of cardboard, as these are too flimsy and a frightened cat may tear its way out. Talk to the cat during your journey home, reassuring it in a calm voice that everything is all right. A kitten that has never been away from its mother before, or an adult that is not used to trav-elling, may be rather anxious, so will probably cry and be restless. A calm voice will help to reassure the cat. As a worried cat may temporarily lose control over its bodily functions, it is a good idea to line the cat carrier with newspapers rather than a clean, new blanket. Alternatively, use an old blanket that can be washed easily.

If properly trained, most dogs will make friends with cats.

On arriving home, bring the cat indoors inside the carrier, and place it in a nice, quiet part of your house. It is a good idea to restrict the cat to one room at first, especially in the case of a kitten. Place a litter tray, a food bowl, a water bowl and perhaps a bed and some toys within easy reach, and then open the door of the cat carrier. Do not attempt to lift the cat (or kitten) out, or even to tempt it out. The cat will feel much more confident and secure if it is allowed to choose when to leave the carrier. If it is reluctant to come out, leave the room, close the door, and let it have some peace and quiet. It will start exploring in its own good time. A kitten will be much more curious than an adult and is likely to settle down sooner. Check on the cat every hour or so, but apart from this you should leave it pretty well alone during the first 24 hours in its new home, unless it appears curious and wants your company. Do make sure that the room is fully secure, and that the cat cannot escape through a window or hide in a small place. A frightened cat can squeeze into the smallest of gaps, and it is not unknown for cats and kittens to disappear up chimneys.

An adult cat, especially a rescued one that may have had bad experiences of people, will take longer to settle than a kitten. Try not to rush things, as this will only frighten the cat even more. Once the cat moves comfortably around the room, and doesn't mind you being there, you can allow it access to the rest of the house. If the cat has been ill-treated previously and is still rather wary of you and your family then patience is the key word. Always talk calmly to the cat, behave in a calm manner when near it (no loud voices and no sudden movements) and do not attempt to pick it up or place it on your lap unless it indicates that this is what it wants.

Cats are independent creatures at the best of times and constant handling of a nervous or unwilling cat will not help gain its confidence at all. Stroke the cat and talk to it, offering it titbits and toys and scratching it in its favourite places (under the chin and behind its ears, for example).

In time you will find that your patience has paid off and, when your cat willingly curls up on your lap without any prompting, you will know that you've cracked it - you're friends!

If you intend to let your cat go outside it is vital that you allow it plenty of time to settle into its new home first. This probably means at least two weeks, possibly longer. Also remember that you should never let your cat out unless it has been neutered and vaccinated. The pros and cons of outdoor versus indoor cats will be discussed in Chapter 3.

Introducing a new cat to a resident cat

If you already have a cat, or several cats, extra care and attention will be needed when you bring your new cat home. Most adult cats will accept the arrival of a kitten into the household eventually, even if it takes a couple of weeks. If your existing cat is already used to other cats the introduction is likely to be an easy one. However, if the first cat has been kept as a single pet for several years, it is unlikely to welcome the new arrival. It may eventually accept the presence of a kitten, and with any luck the two will become friends, but it is also quite possible that the older cat will merely tolerate the kitten. Cats kept on their own for years tend to become 'people-oriented' rather than 'cat-oriented', so it may be worth considering whether it is fair to bring a newcomer into the house. If the cat is less than two years old things will probably work out amicably, but I would be wary of introducing a second cat into a household where the first cat is much older than this.

If your cat is relatively young and known to get on well with other cats the arrival of a new kitten should not cause too much upheaval. Most adult cats will hiss and spit at a new kitten initially, and perhaps occasionally swipe a paw at the inquisitive little creature whom they regard as a little pest. However, it is rare for adult cats to attack kittens outright, and in most cases you will find that the kitten has been fully accepted within a week or even less. Be careful during those first few days, and do not leave the kitten on its own with the adult, just in case.

It is very important to prevent jealousy in your older cat. If a new kitten arrives and you make a great fuss of it the older cat will feel jealous and left out. No matter how difficult it may seem, you must try to pay as much attention as possible to your older cat, spoiling it more than usual and ignoring the little one when the older cat is around. That way, your older cat will feel reassured that it is still 'number one' in your household and that the kitten's arrival has done nothing to change this. My husband thought that I was very cruel when he brought home our second cat, little six-week-old Tippi, a rescued moggy; I virtually ignored her most of the time in favour of our existing cat, Blondie, a Persian. But my strategy worked out, and Blondie very soon realised that she had nothing to fear - she was still number one. In fact, many years later she is still totally convinced that she is my favourite cat, and will never feel threatened by any new arrival, be it cat, dog or baby.

If you already have a cat, or cats, and plan to introduce an adult newcomer, then I would be very wary. Occasionally this may work out, especially if the different cats

The author's daughter meets Hebe, a ginger cat who has appeared on television several times.

Beauty, a silver-tabby kitten who was formerly a stray.

are of the same or very similar breeds, but it can also turn out to be a disaster. Adult cats are much more difficult to introduce to each other than kitten and adult, and it is almost impossible to predict how such an introduction will work out. Doubtless, people manage to do this all the time, but there are also instances when things have gone badly wrong. Somebody I once knew took on several rescued cats, all adults, one at a time. They all seemed to tolerate each other and did not fight for a while. However, they never became real friends, and eventually there was a total breakdown; all the cats started fighting among themselves. It ended with new homes having to be found for all of them. So, to be on the safe side, I would not recommend taking on a adult cat if you already have one.

Introducing cats of different breeds

Odd as it may seem, cats do tend to be rather racist (or perhaps 'breedist') and because of this one should take care not to mix breeds that are too different from each other. Most non-pedigree cats, because of their mixed breeding, mix happily with other non-pedigrees. In any case, if you only have two cats you will probably find that they will get along just fine, no matter how different they are. For instance, a moggy can become firm friends with a pedigree cat of any breed. But (and this is a big 'but') if you keep more than two cats it is important to get the balance of breeds right; otherwise you may end up with one cat that is being pushed aside or even terrorised by the other cats. This has happened in my own multi-breed household of cats and left my husband and me firmly convinced that cats are 'breedist'.

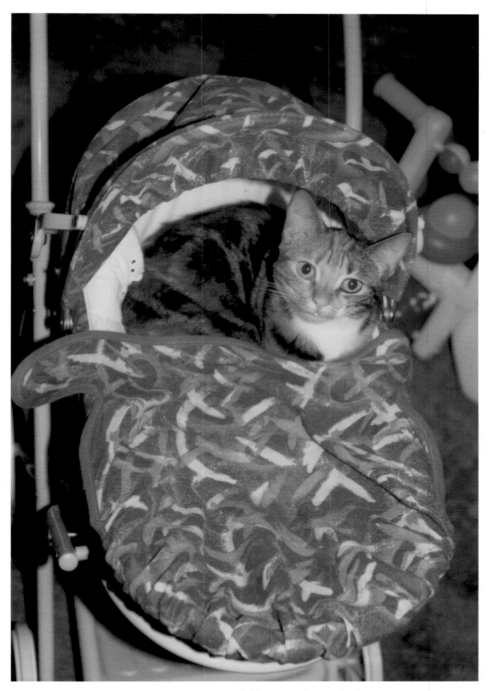

Children must be taught that cats are not toys.

Hamish was a rescued non-pedigree cat. He was half Siamese, half longhaired (probably Colourpoint or Birman). From almost the day we brought him home he was best friends with Tolly, our pedigree Siamese. We never really related their friendship to the fact that they were of similar breeds, especially as they both got on well with our Persians and non-pedigrees too.

However, Hamish had to be put to sleep when he was five years old, and things started to go wrong immediately. Tolly missed his friend desperately. He became quiet and kept to himself, not taking much interest in what was going on around him - quite the opposite of normal Siamese behaviour. Then the other cats started to freeze him out! Our four moggies kept together in pairs: two Tabbies and two Torties. Our Persians and our one Exotic (a shorthaired version of the Persian) kept together in one group. Tolly was not allowed into any of the groups; he was totally ignored.

Eventually, things got so bad that some of the Persians started to attack him viciously, for no apparent reason other than that he was the odd one out, being the only Siamese. We assumed that things would eventually settle again, but after two and a half months nothing had improved. Tolly became more and more depressed, and the attacks on him intensified.

We then decided to buy another Siamese, and brought home a kitten whom we called Sammi. The change was instant; Tolly became his usual happy self again, the other cats stopped attacking him and, after a short while, all the cats were once again mixing with each other, regardless of breed.

These days, our cats are one big happy family and you will often find one Siamese, one Persian and one moggy playing or sleeping together. The lesson we learnt from this was never again to keep one outstandingly different cat, like a Siamese, in a group of Persians and non-pedigrees.

Introducing a cat to other pets

Bringing a cat into a household where pets other than cats already reside is usually marginally easier than introducing a new cat to an existing one. As long as appropriate precautions are taken, and some common sense is used, the introduction of a cat into any household should not be too much of a problem.

Dogs: Introducing a cat into a household in which there is already a dog is preferable to doing things the other way round. A dog usually accepts a new family member more readily and it is much easier to train a dog to behave. It is not true that cats and dogs are natural enemies; they just suffer from certain communication problems. Once these have been overcome, they usually make very good friends. For example, when a cat wags its tail, it means it is uncertain, possibly nervous or angry. A dog wagging its tail displays happiness and friendliness - quite the opposite of the cat.

As you probably will not know what your dog's reaction to a cat will be, you should always take great care when introducing them to each other. If your dog often chases cats you should be wary, but bear in mind that most dogs will chase strange cats outdoors while living in total harmony with a cat at home. A dog will chase anything that moves fast, but there is no space for the cat to run at a great speed in a house.

When your new cat has arrived in your home (or preferably has been allowed to settle for a while in a separate room) you can let the dog and the cat meet. Always make any introductions with the dog on a lead, so that you can control it should this be necessary, but with the cat unrestrained. If you hold the cat in your arms it may panic at being restricted and unable to escape; it will be very upset and frightened. Let the cat approach the dog rather than the other way around. Another good method of introduction is to place the cat in a large indoor pen similar to those used for puppies or kittens (but make sure that it has a roof, as the cat may otherwise climb out). That way the cat and the dog can observe without being able to hurt each other. If the dog and the cat both seem calm you can open the door of the pen and let the cat wander out.

Never leave the cat and the dog shut up together until they have either become friends or learnt to tolerate each other. You can let the cat wander freely, but do restrict the dog to one room. By placing a baby-gate across the door you will stop the dog from moving out of that room but the cat will be able to come and go as it pleases, either by walking through the bars of the gate or by jumping over it. It also helps if the dog is kept in the kitchen, as the cat will then have plenty of raised areas to escape onto if it feels threatened: the sink, a kitchen table or even the cooker. In most cases, the cat and the dog soon settle down together and, before you know it, you will find them sleeping side by side in the dog's bed.

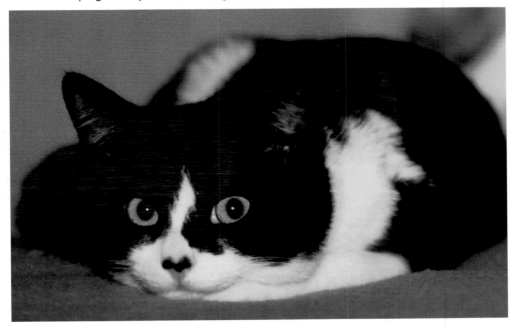

Myrtle looks as though she is ready to pounce on the camera!
Photograph by Anthony Burgess

Most breeds of dog can get on well with cats but, if you happen to own a terrier or a hunting dog such as a greyhound, extra care should be taken. Sadly, dogs do kill cats occasionally, but when this happens it is usually outdoors, by a dog that has the natural instincts to chase and hunt.

Finally, cats can hurt dogs too, particularly by scratching dogs' eyes with their sharp claws. But as long as the cat has a place of safety when it feels threatened, such as a table out of the dog's reach, this is very unlikely to happen. A cat will usually attack only as a last resort. I have twenty cats and four dogs, and they are all the best of friends.

Rabbits: Keeping rabbits and cats rarely causes any problems. The two animals may even become friends. A cat is unlikely to attack a rabbit because most rabbits are far too big for a cat to handle. Also, as most rabbits are kept outdoors in hutches, the cat and the rabbit are not likely to meet eye-to-eye. Be careful if you have baby rabbits, small enough for a cat to kill. In that case you should not let them meet.

Guinea pigs (cavies): Very much the same applies as for rabbits. Cats will usually ignore guinea pigs, as they are too large to be considered prey. The one time to be very careful is when you have baby guinea pigs, which to a cat may resemble rats very closely.

Hamsters, rats, mice and gerbils: The rule here is never to let cats come into close contact with these animals. There are cases where cats have befriended such small animals, but they are a cat's natural prey, and even an indoor cat that has never caught and killed a small animal may eventually be tempted beyond resistance. Always keep animals of this type where the cat cannot get at them, preferably in a separate room with a closed door, or in an outbuilding to which the cat has no access. That the small pet will be kept inside a cage is not necessarily protection enough; the cat can knock the cage over and damage it so that the animal escapes, or someone may forget to close the cage door properly one day.

Cage birds: Small cage birds are also a cat's natural prey and should always be kept out of reach. I have solved this problem by keeping my bird cages on top of tall bookcases, the cages secured to the wall by means of metal hooks. Even if a cat managed to reach the cage on the shelf it would not be able to knock it down and would find it virtually impossible to get the cage open.

Large birds: Birds such as parrots can get on well with cats given time, but in this case it is more a question of protecting the cat from the bird. A parrot's beak could injure a cat badly, so the two should never be left alone unsupervised.

CATS AND CHILDREN

'Animals and children do not mix!' said the visiting midwife when I was expecting my first child, looking disapprovingly at our collection of cats, dogs and smaller animals. She couldn't have been more wrong! My first-born was given her first 'very own' cat at the tender age of six months and has been a committed cat-lover ever since.

It is not so much a case of finding a cat that gets on well with children as of teaching your children how to behave towards cats and how to handle them. It is never too early to start teaching a child these basics, and at around the age of 12 the child should be old enough to understand what it really means. Before this, it is very much a case of supervising the child and the cat when they are together.

Any cat can learn to tolerate and like children as long as it is treated properly by the child. However, it is easier for a young cat or kitten to adjust to the presence of a child than it is for an adult cat that may never have had any experience of children. Never let your child torment the cat; always make sure that the cat is treated with care and affection. Teach the child how to hold it, and explain that pulling its tail will hurt the cat, and then the cat will not like the child. When our first-born, Rebecca, was still a baby, we illustrated this by showing her that a toy cat can be handled roughly and will not mind, but a real cat must always be treated with care. She grew up with our cats and handling them came naturally.

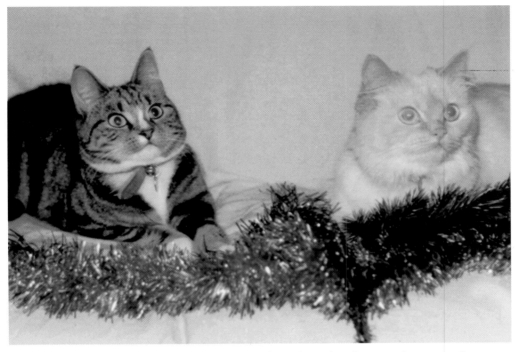

Cats often prefer friends similar to themselves, but Tippi the moggy always liked her Persian friend, Blondie.

No cat will be a health risk to a child as long as it is wormed, de-flead and vaccinated regularly and the cat and its litter tray are kept clean. Always place the litter tray and food bowls where the child can't reach them. Toddlers are notorious for wanting to put everything into their mouths and this may very well include soiled cat litter or cat food. The cat should have its own resting place where the child cannot reach it, so that it knows that it always has a place of peace and quiet to escape to. Likewise, the cat should not be allowed into the child's bedroom.

Do not believe the old tales of cats suffocating babies by sleeping on them; this simply does not happen. However, the cat should be kept out of the child's bedroom for reasons of hygiene. It is good for the cat to know that this room is out of bounds; just as the cat has its own resting place where the child cannot reach it, the child has his or hers.

chapter three
general care

INDOOR OR OUTDOOR CAT?

Most people would not think of addressing this question, as the general opinion seems to be that all cats should be allowed to go out. However, it is not quite as simple as this. Many cats, especially non-pedigrees, have a natural urge to go outside, establish a territory and hunt for such prey as birds and mice. They may not be happy kept indoors all their lives. Other cats, especially pedigrees that have been bred indoors for generations, have no wish whatsoever to go out and are much happier staying indoors. They will also be much safer. There is no need to abandon any idea of owning a cat just because you happen to live in a flat on the tenth floor or in a house near a very busy road. You can keep an indoor cat, provided that you choose your cat carefully. It is not true that it is cruel to keep a cat as an indoor pet.

Even if you happen to live in a house with a nice garden, far away from busy roads, there are many aspects to consider before letting your cat out. The dangers to an outdoor cat are numerous. In Sweden, where I was born, a survey was once conducted to find the average lifespans of outdoor and indoor cats. It was found that the average lifespan of a cat that was allowed outdoor access was around two years. For a cat kept exclusively indoors it was nearer to 15 years. That says quite a bit about the dangers that outdoor cats will inevitably face.

Right: A floor-to-ceiling 'cat tree' is greatly appreciated.

Consider the following:

- Any cat allowed outdoors will be at great risk from any of the incurable cat diseases that usually spread via saliva. These include Feline Leukaemia Virus (FeLV), Feline Immunodeficiency Virus (FIV) and Feline Infectious Peritonitis (FIP). FeLV can now be vaccinated against, but there is no vaccine and no cure for the other diseases. (Read further on this subject in Chapter 7.)
- A cat can get lost or stolen.
- A cat can get run over and killed.
- A cat could get killed by a dog or a fox.

On considering all these points one realises how extremely dangerous it can be to let a cat roam freely outdoors. However, as there are cats that would be genuinely unhappy living their lives permanently indoors (especially adult cats that have always had outdoor access), it is impossible to say point blank that all cats should be kept indoors.

If you decide to let your cat go out:
- Do you live in a reasonably quiet area, away from busy roads?
- Do you have neighbours who will not mind if the cat occasionally visits their garden?
- Have you fitted a cat-flap to your door so that the cat can let itself in or out, or is there access through an open window or similar for the cat to get in if you are out? If not, is there anywhere in your garden where your cat could possibly shelter should the weather turn bad?

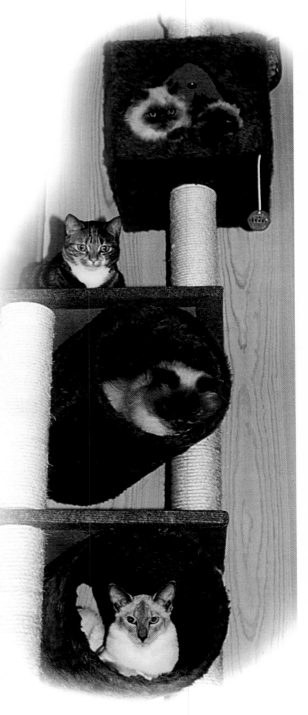

- Is your cat fully vaccinated and neutered? Never allow an unneutered cat to go out. A tom (male) will get into numerous serious fights with other tomcats, is likely to stray far away from home (possibly never to return) and will sire many kittens that will end up as unwanted cats or strays. A queen (female) will mate as soon as she starts calling (coming into season), ultimately producing unplanned kittens for which you will probably have great difficulty in finding homes. She may also have been mated by a tom that carries disease, thus catching serious, life-threatening diseases herself.
- Are you prepared to spend extra time on the cat? An outdoor cat is more likely to catch parasites and will need treatment for these. Any longhaired cat will need extra grooming, as a cat that roams around outdoors will inevitably end up with dirty and matted fur if it is not groomed regularly and more often than an indoor cat.
- Have you considered identification? Any outdoor cat should bear some sort of identification in case it gets lost. This could be in the form of a collar with an engraved disc (the collar being partly elasticated to allow the cat to escape should the collar get caught on something), a microchip implant under the cat's skin, or a tattoo in the ear. The collar and disc is by far the most common means of identification. It has certain advantages: people spotting the collar will realise immediately that the cat is owned by somebody; the collar usually has a bell that will warn birds that a cat is around; and if you buy a reflective collar the cat can be seen in the dark by motorists. One disadvantage is that a cat can lose its collar. The microchip method is fairly expensive, cannot be seen by the naked eye, and has to be implanted by a vet. Tattooing of cats in Great Britain is still fairly rare, but does exist, and is widespread in other countries. A tattoo can be seen clearly by anyone, and cannot be removed, so will act as a deterrent to cat thieves.

If you decide to keep your cat permanently indoors:

- Is your cat either happy to stay in (unwilling to go out) or a kitten that has not yet got used to the idea of spending time outdoors?
- Are you prepared for the extra work involved in cleaning out litter trays regularly?
- Will you provide your cat with a stimulating environment, which must include toys, scratching posts (preferably of the kind that the cat can climb) and companionship? All indoor cats will be happier if they have another feline companion, but this is especially important if the owner goes out to work for several hours a day.

If you still cannot decide whether to go for the indoor or outdoor approach, there are options that are somewhere between the two. You can buy or construct a large wire run (with a shelter) for your cat in the garden, so that it can be left outdoors safely for periods of time. You can 'cat-proof' your garden, virtually turning it into one large run. (This will have to include some sort of a roof, or a fence that slopes inwards so that the cat can't scale it, as cats are very good climbers.) If you live in a flat with a balcony, you can make the balcony cat-proof by fitting wire netting, and then the cat can spend time out there whenever it wishes. Finally, some cats can adapt to walking on a harness and lead if trained to do this as kittens, and that way you can safely take your cat for a walk.

HOUSE TRAINING

Unlike puppies, kittens do not need formal house training from their owners. Their mother teaches them to be clean as early as four weeks. If the queen is an indoor cat with access to a litter tray, she will show her kittens how to use the tray and they will copy her. If she is outdoors, she will probably teach the kittens to use earth in some secluded space. If this is the case (and you may not know for sure when you acquire your kitten or cat) then the kitten will never have been used to a litter tray. However, it is perfectly natural for any cat to relieve itself in soil or sand so, as long as you show your new kitten or cat where its litter tray is kept, it should use this without any further prompting. If you live in a large house, make sure you supply your kitten with more than one litter tray so that there is always one within easy reach. The same rule applies if you keep more than one cat.

GROOMING

How much grooming, and of what kind, a non-pedigree cat needs depends on the cat's coat. An ordinary, shorthaired cat does not need much in the way of grooming. Most cats are very clean creatures that spend hours grooming themselves and avoid getting dirty whenever possible. If you have more than one cat, you will also find that the cats spend a large proportion of time grooming each other. This process helps to remove loose, dead hair from the cat's coat. It also stimulates blood circulation and keeps the coat clean.

If your cat is shorthaired, good at keeping itself clean, and not in moult, the occasional going over with a brush will be all that is needed. If the cat is moulting and losing large quantities of fur, you can speed up the process by brushing or combing the cat daily. If your cat has fleas you will need to treat the condition with a spray or similar insecticide and then remove dead fleas and flea dirt with a fine-toothed flea comb. A cat that is allowed outdoors will get dirtier than an indoor cat, and so may need brushing or combing more frequently.

Most longhaired non-pedigree cats are what is described as 'semi-longhaired'. This means that their fur is neither as long nor as fine as that of the true longhaired cat, the Persian, so they will not need as much grooming. However, grooming is still necessary: no longhaired cat is capable of grooming itself effectively. If it is not combed by its owner, knots and matted areas of fur will start to develop sooner or later. This will be very uncomfortable for the cat, and can cause skin problems.

A longhaired non-pedigree cat will need grooming once or twice a week; the fuller the coat, the more grooming will be needed. Use a fine-toothed metal comb, as a brush will not reach through the fur. Comb the cat all over, paying particular attention to the areas where knots usually form: behind the ears, under the legs, on the stomach, on the 'trousers' on the hind legs, and in the ruff on the cat's chest. An outdoor longhaired cat is much more likely to get matted fur than an indoor one.

If you have a cat whose long coat mats very easily, it is a good idea to sprinkle the coat regularly, perhaps a few times a week, with baby talcum powder, gently rubbing it into the cat's coat. You can then either brush it out, or leave it in. As long as you make sure not to get any powder inside the cat's eyes, ears or nose, and only use non-perfumed baby powder, this process is harmless and will help to keep the cat's coat free of grease and more manageable. All breeders of Persians do this. It can also be an ideal way to clean your longhaired cat if it is not dirty enough or you do not have time to give it a full bath.

If your cat has had diarrhoea, then its furry hind legs will probably be very stained and dirty. Rinse the fur carefully with lukewarm water, rub dry with a towel, and then sprinkle liberally with talcum powder. Once the coat is dry, brush out the powder, and most of the residual dirt will follow. It will also make your cat smell clean.

Bathing

A clean, shorthaired cat that is an indoor pet, not intended for showing, may keep so clean that it will never need a bath. In fact, my own first moggy, Felix, the tabby, has never had a bath during all his 17 years! Other cats may need an occasional bath, and longhaired non-pedigree cats will definitely benefit from regular baths, every two months or so. It is true that most cats dislike water, and some cats will never fully accept being bathed, but a cat that has been used to baths since kittenhood will accept the process without too much fuss. A cat should be bathed if it looks dirty, if the coat has become very greasy, if it has any skin complaint that necessitates a medical bath, or if you intend to show it. A longhaired cat which has started to develop knots will usually be greatly improved by having a bath, as all excess grease in the coat will be washed away so that knots will not form as easily.

To bath your cat, place it in the kitchen sink, a suitable large bowl, or the bath. Always make sure that the surface on which the cat is standing is not slippery, as this will make the cat panic. A rubber bath mat in the bath is ideal. Most cats will also feel safer if they have somewhere to rest their front paws, such as the edge of a bowl. If the cat is not used to being bathed, the gentlest method is to fill the bath or bowl with enough lukewarm water to reach the cat's stomach. Then you can either pour water all over your cat gently (taking great care to avoid the eyes, nose and ears) from a small jug or squeeze a sponge over it. Make sure that the cat's fur is thoroughly soaked.

Now apply the shampoo. You can use a gentle baby shampoo, but never use a shampoo intended for adult humans, as this could be toxic if swallowed. There are numerous shampoos especially for cats, and these are available from pet shops or veterinary surgeries. Avoid using a shampoo for dogs unless it clearly states that it is suitable for both dogs and cats: certain shampoos for dogs may be poisonous to cats, especially the insecticidal ones, such as flea shampoo.

Gently rub the shampoo into the cat's fur, then rinse the fur with clean water. Do not leave any traces of shampoo in the cat's coat. Once the coat is rinsed clean, gently squeeze the cat's fur to remove some of the excess water, and then lift it out of the bath, rubbing it well with a towel. Do not stop until the cat's fur is as dry as possible. Most cats are very frightened of a hair-dryer but this is the best way of getting a cat dry if it will let you. If not, confine the cat to one warm room (preferably where it can rest in front of a fire or radiator) until it is dry.

Soon your cat will be used to being bathed, so the whole process can be speeded up by using a hand-held shower in the bath to soak the cat and rinse it clean of shampoo.

Tooth care

All cats get tartar on their teeth sooner or later. This may occur when the cat is only a year old, and you should always watch out for it. A cat whose teeth have accumulated an excessive amount of tartar will have bad breath and suffer from gum disease, with red, inflamed gums that may even bleed. Eventually it will find it difficult or impossible to eat, and may lose teeth.

The way to prevent the build-up of tartar is to give the cat plenty of hard food to chew, such as dry cat food or even lightly boiled pig's heart. It is interesting to note that outdoor cats which catch and eat birds and rodents often have remarkably clean teeth. If possible, regularly remove tartar from the cat's teeth yourself. I use a toothscrape (as used by dentists) to scrape it off my cat's teeth every other

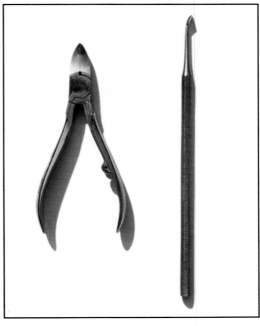

Clawcutters and toothscrape.

month, before the problem becomes severe. The sooner it is removed, the easier it will be. Not all cats allow their owners to do this, but I find that most accept the process if you start when they are young and involve a second person as a helper to hold the cat for you. If you cannot do this yourself you must let a vet remove the tartar from the cat's teeth at regular intervals; ask your vet how often this is necessary. Most vets will examine a cat's teeth when it arrives for its annual booster vaccination, and will tell the owner whether any tartar needs removing. Vets usually put cats under general anaesthetic to remove tartar, which means that the process cannot be done too often, although some vets prefer just to give the cat a sedative.

It is possible to buy for your pets special toothbrushes and toothpastes designed to reduce the incidence of tartar. Ask your vet for advice.

Claws

Normally, a cat's claws will not need to be trimmed. If your cat is allowed to go out it may be best to leave the claws alone, as the cat will need its sharp-tipped claws for defence or climbing. An indoor cat will benefit from having its claws trimmed every couple of weeks or so. This will help to reduce damage to your furniture, and it will also make it easier for your cat to play with you without scratching you accidentally. Any cat entered into a show should have had its claws trimmed beforehand.

To trim your cat's claws you can use a pair of nail clippers or scissors intended for humans, although you can buy special cat ones from pet shops. Gently press the top of the paw to make the claws protrude, then snip off the tip of the claw - no more.

De-clawing involves the actual removal of all of the claw and the first toe-joint. It is never carried out in Great Britain; vets will not perform the operation and a de-clawed cat would be disqualified from any show. It does occur elsewhere in the world.

Ears

A healthy cat will not normally need any attention to its ears. As long as the ear appears clean, with no discharge or unpleasant smell, and the cat does not scratch its ears or shake its head, the ears are best left alone. Over-zealous cleaning of cats' ears will only promote the production of too much wax, which may actually cause problems.

Some cats produce more earwax than others. This is particularly true of longhairs because their ears, being so furry, are warmer than those of shorthairs. If you see a greasy, waxy substance, normally brown in colour, on the cat's outer ear, wipe it away with a damp piece of cotton wool or a special ear wipe, available from pet shops and vets. Do not attempt to clean inside the ear unless the cat is showing obvious signs of discomfort, such as scratching it. If the ear leaks any liquid, or has a dark, almost brown, crusty matter inside it, the cat should be taken to a vet for examination. This often indicates ear mites or an infection, which will need special drops prescribed by a vet. (See Chapter 7: Health care.)

NEUTERING

All non-pedigree cats should be neutered; this cannot be stressed strongly enough. No non-pedigree cat should be bred from, as there are already thousands waiting for homes. (See Chapter 5: Raising Kittens.) If you allow your non-pedigree cat to breed you will only increase the number of unwanted cats. Even if good homes are found for your kittens, no cat should be bred from unless it has been tested for disease, and this is seldom the case with non-pedigree cats. If non-pedigree kittens were raised properly, the expense would be great enough to warrant very high prices indeed for the kittens, almost as high as those charged for pedigree cats. Then nobody would buy them, as cheap or free moggy kittens are always available.

It is not true that all female cats should be allowed to have a litter before they are neutered. I would actually go as far as to say that it will do your female cat more harm than good. Many female cats that have been allowed to breed before being neutered are broody for the rest of their lives.

Quite apart from not wishing to increase the number of unwanted kittens, there are medical reasons for having your cat neutered. A spayed female is less likely to develop mammary tumours, and will never have such problems as womb infections. Male cats will be much less inclined to fight and wander, so will be at considerably less risk from diseases such as FeLV and FIV.

Finally, a neutered male cat will become much more affectionate and easier to handle than an entire tom, and he will be far less likely to develop antisocial habits such as spraying urine either indoors or outdoors, which is a way of marking territory. The same goes for females: a queen who isn't spayed is likely to spray, although not to the same extent as a tom. She will also come into season (call) every spring and, if not mated, will continue to do so every three weeks. At such times she will call (scream) loudly for a mate, she will roll on the floor, go off her food, and may very well take to spraying. If this is allowed to continue for too long, she may develop fallopian cysts. Female cats can be put on the feline version of the pill, or receive regular contraceptive injections, but this practice is not recommended. Such treatment is usually given only to pedigree queens from whom their owners wish to breed at a later date. Even then it should only be seen as a last resort. A queen on the pill, or who receives contraceptive injections, is likely sooner or later to develop pyometra, an inflamed womb, which will mean that she will have to be spayed anyway. In any case, it is easy to forget to give your cat her pill, which may set her calling again.

As far as neutering is concerned, ask your vet when it should be done. Opinions vary. Most tend to recommend the age of six months for both sexes. Some cats mature early, and can be neutered earlier; others take a long time to develop and can be left until they are 10 or 12 months old. Your vet will be able to advise you.

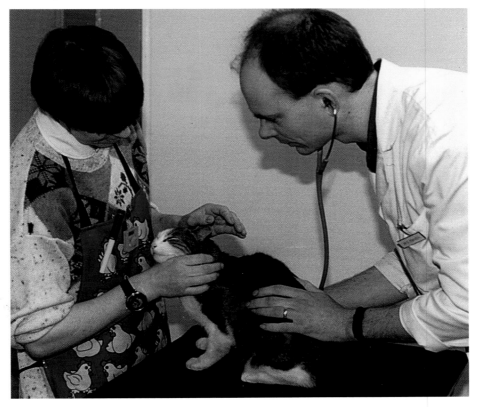

Your cat will need regular vaccinations.

VACCINATION

All cats, indoor and outdoor alike, need to receive regular vaccinations. It is no good believing that your cat will be safe simply because it does not go out. Viruses can be transferred to your cat from outdoors from your shoes or clothing. All cats should be vaccinated against Feline Infectious Enteritis (Feline Panleucopaenia) and against Feline Rhinotraceitis and Feline Calicivirus (known collectively as 'cat flu').

The first injection is usually given at the age of nine weeks (no earlier) or whenever you get your kitten if it is not vaccinated already, followed by a second one at 12 weeks. The first time a cat or kitten is vaccinated two injections are necessary to secure immunity. After that, one booster injection is necessary annually, and it is important not to forget this. Many vets these days send out reminders when cats are due for their boosters, which is an excellent idea.

Metal or earthenware bowls are best for your cat's food and water.

It is also possible to vaccinate your cat against Feline Leukaemia Virus (FeLV) and Feline Chlamydia, although this is not yet carried out routinely. If your cat goes outdoors it is probably a good idea to discuss the option of further vaccinations with your vet. If it is an indoor cat, who has no contact with cats that are allowed outside, you can probably safely leave these vaccinations. Again, ask your vet for advice.

WORMING

All outdoor cats will need regular worming, and most indoor cats, too. Roundworms and tapeworms are the most usual internal parasites in cats, and worming against these should be carried out at least every three months. (See Chapter 7: Health care.) An unwormed cat will be an unhealthy cat, and a cat with roundworms also poses a slight health risk to humans.

The roundworm *Toxocara cati* lays eggs that are present in the cat's faeces. If allowed to mature, usually within a period of two weeks, these eggs will develop into parasites which can infect humans if accidentally swallowed. This is unlikely to occur indoors as an indoor cat will have its litter tray cleaned regularly and, in any case, is less likely to catch roundworm in the first place. An outdoor cat, however, must be wormed regularly, especially as outdoor cats may use children's uncovered sand pits as litter trays. Any roundworm treatment should be administered twice, with two weeks between each worming.

Tapeworms are not harmful to people but can still cause health problems for the cat. Tapeworms are usually contracted through fleas, the cat accidentally swallowing them when licking itself. As indoor cats also get fleas, all cats are susceptible to tapeworm. If a cat has contracted tapeworm, not only must it be wormed, but a de-fleaing programme must also be embarked upon, as treatment is useless otherwise.

EQUIPMENT

There is some equipment that you definitely need for your cat, some that may be useful, and some that is nice to have but not necessary. Here you will find a list of the most common equipment for pet cats.

Food and water bowls

These are essential items, as all cats eat and drink. The best type of food bowl is the metal one, which is easy to keep clean and non-breakable. Earthenware bowls can also be used. Plastic ones are very popular but can contain colouring to which some cats are allergic. As they are used, they will get scratched and chewed, making it difficult to clean them hygienically.

Litter tray with cat litter

Any cat that spends time indoors will need a litter tray. Even if your cat goes out, you may need a litter tray for night time, when the cat should be kept indoors. Litter trays come in many shapes and sizes. There are plain, simple ones that are just plastic trays. If you choose one of these, pick one that is as deep as possible, as this will prevent too much litter from spilling out. A slightly more sophisticated version is the litter tray with a removable lip, which is there to prevent litter from being kicked out. Hooded litter trays are ideal for cats that like their privacy,

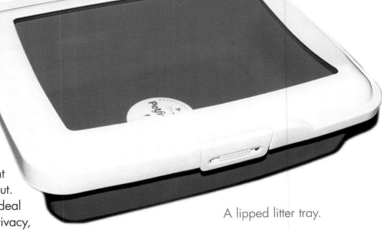

A lipped litter tray.

and they also serve to reduce the smell and keep the litter in. There are also hooded litter trays that come complete with a filter on the top to reduce bad smells more effectively. New arrivals on the market are electronic litter trays that work extra hard at eliminating bad smells, and now there are even self-cleaning ones! There are also disposable litter trays, which you throw away when they are dirty. Choose the tray which best suits you, your cat, and your pocket.

There are just as many different types of cat litter. These include earth-based litters, wood-based litters and paper-based litters. Some form clumps which can be removed once the litter is wet. Again, the choice of cat litter is very much a personal one. You may have to try a few different types before you find the one that seems to suit you and your cat best. For example, some cats don't like the feel of one particular litter, but do not mind another. White litter can often be rather dusty, and this may irritate a sensitive cat's eyes. Wood-based cat litter often disintegrates into fine sawdust when wet, and this may cling to the fur of a longhaired cat.

Whichever litter you choose, make sure that it is always kept as clean as possible. Ideally, any faeces should be removed almost as soon as they appear, and the entire litter tray should be emptied and washed out as soon as it appears dirty. It is impossible to state categorically how often this will be: it depends on such factors as the size of the tray, the size and number of cats using it and the type of litter used. Never leave a dirty litter tray down, as cats are such clean animals that they seldom use a dirty litter tray but may end up using your best carpet instead!

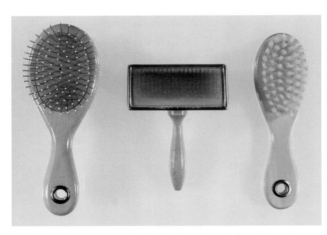

Double-sided brush, slicker brush and bristle brush.

The litter tray should be placed in a secluded place where the cat can have some peace and quiet. A corner in the kitchen or in the bathroom is usually ideal. Never place a litter tray near to where the cat eats, as cats will not relieve themselves near their feeding place.

Brushes and combs

For the shorthaired cat, you will usually need only one soft brush or a slicker brush (for moulting times) and a flea comb, preferably metal. For a longhaired cat, a metal comb with medium-sized teeth will be necessary, together with a brush and a flea comb.

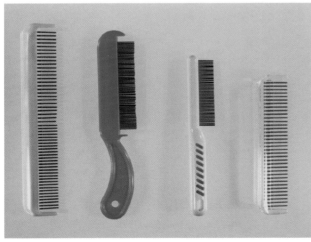

Wide-toothed metal comb, flea comb, fine-toothed comb and small wide- toothed comb.

Cat-carrier

A cat-carrier is a 'must'; there will always be times when you will need to transport your cat. As I have mentioned earlier, never trust cardboard boxes or carriers made of cardboard, as determined or frightened cats can claw their way out of these. There are many excellent cat carriers on the market, available from pet shops and veterinary surgeries. The best type is the plastic carrier which opens either by a door at the side or by lifting up the top. Cats feel secure in this type of carrier, and cannot escape. All-wire carriers can be rather frightening for nervous cats and are no protection against bad weather. I have seen cats that have got their teeth caught in the wire and injured themselves.

A good-quality cat-carrier is a 'must' for when you need to transport your cat.

Six-month-old Roquette enjoying a lazy time. Photograph by Anthony Burgess

All cats love to play, and there are many toys to choose from.

Beds

Strictly speaking, a bed for your cat is not really necessary and, having bought an expensive cat bed, you may well find your cat curled up on your bed, on the furniture, on the carpet, or even in an old cardboard box. Cats will sleep wherever they please, and it is virtually impossible to convince them to sleep elsewhere. So the long and the short of it is, buy a special bed for your cat if you want to, but don't be disappointed if it is not used. Some cats love special cat beds; others do not.

Toys

Most cats, especially kittens, love toys to play with. Single cats should certainly be given toys, to relieve boredom and (hopefully) to stop them from playing with any item that they can find. There are numerous cat toys to be found in pet shops. Some contain catnip, a herb that greatly excites the cat and keeps it playing with the toy for hours on end. If you buy toys from a pet shop, check carefully that they do not contain any small parts that easily can be removed and accidentally swallowed by the cat. Unfortunately, pets' toys, unlike children's toys, are not covered by legislation regarding their safety. If you do not want to spend too much money, a table tennis ball makes an excellent toy, as does a piece of screwed-up paper, a pine cone or a toilet roll centre.

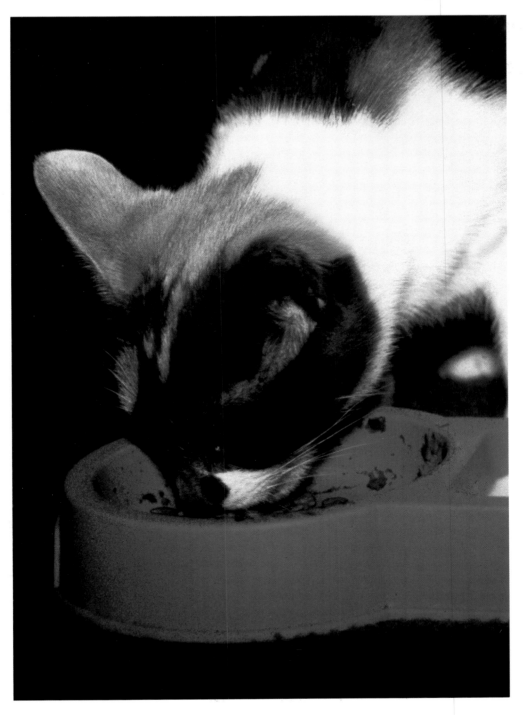

Plastic containers are a popular choice; but do replace them when they get scratched.

Scratching posts

Any indoor cat will need a scratching post; otherwise your furniture will soon be ripped to pieces. Cats need to scratch, both to exercise their claws and to assert their dominance. If a cat has been introduced to the idea of a scratching post as a young kitten, then hopefully it will always prefer this to your furniture. An adult cat that has not been given a scratching post until later in life may be difficult to convince.

Scratching posts can be very simple or very elaborate. The simplest and cheapest kind is a piece of cardboard impregnated with catnip. Most cats love to scratch these, but they do not last long and have to be replaced regularly. The most common type of scratching post is made of wood covered in tough carpet, either in the shape of a post, or in more elaborate designs such as shelves for the cat to climb on, houses, or tunnels. The best of these have posts covered in sisal rope, which cats love to scratch, and which also makes them easy to climb. It is possible to get this type of scratching post in almost any size, from a small one about 30cm high to one that actually reaches all the way up to your ceiling. Pick the one you can afford.

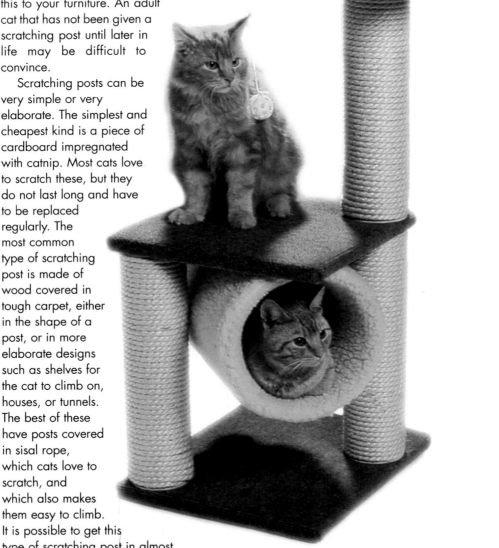

A scratching post will save wear and tear on your furniture.

This is all the equipment that is needed for the average pet cat. If you want to show your cat you will need special show equipment, but this will be covered in a later chapter. (See Chapter 6: Showing Non-pedigree Cats.) Further useful but non-essential items include the automatic cat feeder, which will feed your cat at set times if you have to leave it alone for a day, and cat-flaps, which come in many different shapes and sizes.

GOING ON HOLIDAY

Even cat owners are likely to want to go on holiday sometimes, and the question that immediately arises then is what to do with the cat or cats. Some people take their cats on holiday with them. In Great Britain this will have to mean a holiday within the country, as it is not possible to bring a cat back into the country without putting it into quarantine for six months. Anyway, I think that most cats are better off being cared for in a cattery, in their own home or with a friend or relative rather than having to put up with travelling.

The best place for your cat during your holiday is undoubtedly a good-quality, licensed boarding cattery. In a good cattery your cat will receive the best of care and veterinary attention will be available immediately should the need arise. Your cat will also be secure and very unlikely to be able to escape and wander off, always a risk if somebody else is looking after it in your own home. So, how do you find a good boarding cattery? Never take a proprietor's word that his establishment is excellent, or believe outright what you read in advertisements.

Ask your vet and other cat-owning friends for recommendations, as these will usually be your very best references. Most important of all, visit the cattery before you decide whether to leave your cat there. For your own peace of mind, check that everything appears to be in order.

Ask as many questions as you like:

- How often are the cats fed?
- Will they feed your cat on its normal food so that it will not suffer from an upset stomach due to a change of diet?
- Do they insist on vaccinated cats only?
- Are the individual pens large enough?
- Are they airy, but still warm enough for cold weather? (Many have heated cabins.)
- If you have two cats, can they share?
- Are the pens secure? All boarding catteries should have some sort of safety corridor so that, if a cat runs out of its pen, it will not be able to get outside and escape.
- Are the pens placed a metre or so apart, or are the dividing walls solid, so that the cats can't come into contact with each other, or spread disease by sneezing?

Do not be afraid to ask many questions; any good boarding cattery will be happy to answer them. Always beware of places in which certain questions are avoided and areas are fenced off to stop you from seeing them. Some unscrupulous catteries have a few show pens in front, in which they promise the customer that the cat will be kept, and then, once the owner is out of sight, they will put it in a much smaller, rabbit-hutch-style pen at the back, away from public view.

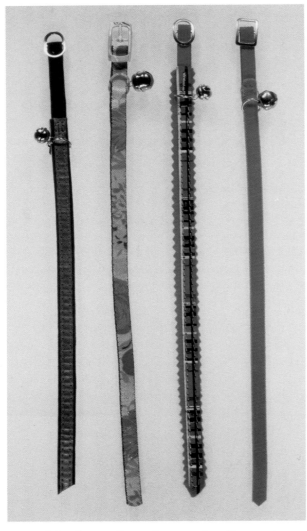

Finally, if at all possible, choose a cattery that boards cats only, not cats and dogs. It can be very unnerving for a cat to spend a week or more in a place where there is constant barking, especially if it is not used to dogs.

The second best option for cat care when you go on holiday is to find somebody reliable to stay in your house and look after your cat. Maybe a friend can do this, or a relative. Failing this, there are agencies that will place people in homes, caring for both the pets and the house. This has the advantage of keeping your home secure while you are away but you must take the risk that your cat may not like the idea of a stranger in your home and, if allowed out, may simply wander off.

Your third option is to find a trusted friend or relative who will look after your cat in their own home. If you decide on this, make absolutely sure that your cat will not be allowed out. In an unfamiliar area, cared

From left: flea collar, elasticated collar and two decorative collars. A useful form of identification is a collar with an engraved disc in case your cat gets lost.

for by people that are not its family, your cat may get confused and try to return home.

Wherever you decide to leave your cat, make sure you leave explicit instructions on the cat's diet, any peculiar or special habits and any medication it may be on, as well as your vet's telephone number and a contact number for you. Try to leave your cat with some familiar object, such as its own bed and toys or an old jumper of yours that has your scent on it; this will reassure the cat.

No matter how much you buy for your cat, there is no substitute for love.

chapter

four
feeding

Feeding a cat or kitten is more complicated than you might think. Cats have unique nutritional requirements. They are obligate carnivores, which means it is literally essential that they eat meat. A cat cannot survive on a low-protein or vegetarian diet, whereas the dog, which is omnivorous, can survive on a completely meat-free diet if it has to. An adult cat needs to consume twice as much protein as a dog, whilst growing kittens need twice as much again.

Nowadays, there are many 'complete' cat foods on the market. Many are very good, containing all the nutritional requirements in a cat's general diet necessary to keep it healthy for many years to come, but some are not so good. Three or four decades ago, when most pet cats were fed largely on table scraps, the cats themselves supplemented their diet by catching and eating rats and mice. These days, many cats are kept permanently indoors and do not have access to such delicacies. Even cats who go outdoors may not necessarily have a chance to catch rats and mice, as pest control techniques are much more effective nowadays. Therefore, it is absolutely essential that you provide your cat with a good, well-balanced diet.

The feline intestine is adapted for a diet high in fat and protein, the sort of diet which is high in energy but low in bulk. Proteins are essential for building tissue, resisting disease and maintaining a luxuriant coat and strong muscles and bones. Unlike dogs, cats are unable to manufacture certain essential nutrients themselves, so it is extremely important that these nutrients are present in your cat's diet. Proteins are made up of amino acids. Cats need up to 20 different amino acids to be able to manufacture the proteins that their bodies need. Ten of these amino acids can be manufactured by the cat's own bodily system, but the other 10 must be taken in as part of its normal diet.

One of the most vital amino acids is Taurine. This is essential to cats and can be derived only from animal tissue; in other words, meat. If the cat does not get an adequate supply of Taurine, then chronic Taurine deficiency will result, generating a number of unpleasant effects. The most widely known of these is blindness, but others include heart problems, brain damage and infertility.

Cats are incapable of manufacturing some essential fatty acids, so again these must be present in the diet. Fats are used as a source of energy other than protein and are very useful to the cat in the prevention and treatment of skin diseases.

Vitamins A and E are needed to ensure the normal functioning of the cat's membranes. Vitamin A can be found only in animal tissue. The various B Vitamins are needed by many enzymes in the cat's body. Liver contains high levels of Vitamins A and B and is a common ingredient in commercial cat food. However, fresh liver is addictive to cats. Long term feeding of liver can result in problems caused by Vitamin A Toxicity: the cat is literally poisoned by too much Vitamin A entering its body.

Of the B Vitamins, Thiamine is essential. Thiamine deficiency causes brain damage, and Thiamine can be destroyed by acidity and heat. The Thiamine-destroying enzyme Thiaminase can be found in certain types of raw fish. Always remember to cook any fish that you feed to your cat.

Vitamin K is necessary to blood clotting, while Vitamin D is involved in bone metabolism and healthy growth.

Cats do not actually need fibre in their diet, although a little fibre intake can be useful, helping to alleviate constipation and ridding the cat of furballs in its stomach. Too much fibre will reduce the cat's ability to digest food, leading to water retention in the cat's intestines. Less water will be disposed of as urine and what urine there is will be very concentrated. This may result in Feline Urological Syndrome (FUS). (See Chapter 7: Health care.)

The cat has no specific need for carbohydrate, but this is often present in cat food in the form of cereal. Cereal is a cheap but inferior source of energy, as the proteins present in cereal lack the specific amino acids which the cat needs to manufacture protein within its body.

A cat's absorption of minerals varies with the type of food it is given. A diet rich in fat will lead to a reduced absorption of calcium and trace elements. Conversely, too much calcium can retard a kitten's growth and reduce the absorption of other elements, such as phosphorus, copper, zinc and iron. Too much phosphorus can result in calcium deficiency and kidney problems. Too much magnesium may also result in FUS (see above). Too much sodium can lead to kidney problems. Diets high in ash content should be avoided in cats that are known to be prone to FUS.

CHOOSING YOUR CAT'S FOOD

This may seem a daunting prospect, but don't worry; there are many excellent cat foods on the market. To start with, always try to adhere to what a kitten or cat has been used to eating at its original home. You can start to phase in any modifications gradually once the cat has settled into its new home.

So, should you give your cat canned food, a complete dried food, or both? Most cats are fed on canned food and do very well on it. The main difference between canned and dry foods is the water content. All cans of cat food contain at least 75% water, whereas dry food contains 8-12%. Dry food may be more economical and take up less storage space, and the cat needs to eat less of it to gain all its nutritional requirements. However - and most importantly - if a cat is fed on dry food only, it is essential to ensure that the cat drinks enough water.

Water is the cat's most essential nutrient. Deprived of water, a cat will soon become dehydrated and die. A cat fed on canned food will automatically have a high water intake and will very seldom be seen to drink. That said, fresh drinking water must always be available. Water is far better than milk for adult cats. Milk is best given to kittens and pregnant or nursing queens only. Special 'feline milks' aimed at adult cats and kittens are available in pet shops and supermarkets.

Always read the label on the packaging of the food you are considering. The ingredients are listed in descending order of weight, and therefore content. It is worth bearing in mind that meat and meat derivatives contain water and may be heavier than cereals, when in fact cereal may be the main ingredient.

HOW MUCH FOOD

How much food your cat actually needs depends upon the quality of the food. The feeding recommendations on the can or packet of food should be seen as guidelines only, as all cats are individuals and will need varying amounts of food.

An adult cat (from the age of about nine months) will need two meals per day: morning and evening. Many cats like to feed on and off all day, thus making one meal last several hours. This should be actively discouraged, especially if canned food is given, as it will soon go off at ordinary room temperature. Remove the bowl of food as soon as the cat has finished eating, whether all the food is gone or not. The cat will soon learn to eat all its food at once. If you have more than one cat they will finish their food quickly because, if they don't, somebody else will finish it up for them!

It is important never to spoil your cat. Many cats prefer one sort of food and may refuse to eat anything else at first. If the owner gives in to the cat and feeds it only the preferred food, the result will be a very spoilt and picky cat. This is to be avoided at all costs, as feeding only one sort of food could lead to serious deficiencies.

FEEDING GROWING KITTENS

Feeding a kitten is a very different matter from feeding a fully-grown cat. A growing kitten has up to three times the energy requirement of an adult cat. It is essential that growing kittens receive adequate nutrition if they are to have the best possible chance of growing into healthy adults.

Kittens have extremely small stomachs and it is therefore vitally important that they receive a diet high in protein and energy. If the food is of poor quality the kitten may be physically unable to eat enough of it to satisfy its growth requirements. In such a case, the kitten may develop a pot-bellied appearance and grow very slowly, with poor muscular and skeletal development and decreased resistance to infection.

By far the best diet for a kitten is a specially formulated kitten food, which can be found in either canned or dry form. Kitten foods are high in protein and fat, which means that the kitten does not need to eat much of the food to receive all the energy it needs. In addition to the kitten food, specially formulated milk for kittens should be given in preference to water.

Kittens from 12 weeks (when weaned) up to approximately five or six months should be given at least four meals a day. Older kittens, from five or six months to nine months, should receive three meals a day. In adulthood, from nine months onwards, two meals a day will be sufficient.

Ideally, growing kittens should be allowed to eat as much as they want.

CATS WITH SPECIAL DIETARY NEEDS

Pregnant or lactating queens will need more energy than other adult cats. Three to four meals a day will be necessary, with special 'cat milk' as a drink.

Old and sick cats, such as those with kidney problems, may need special diets. This is something to discuss carefully with your vet. Most good vets sell diets manufactured for cats with specific needs.

SUPPLEMENTS AND TREATS

Vitamin and mineral supplements can be found in plentiful supply in pet shops. The average adult cat receiving a good diet will not need any of these, but added vitamins and calcium may be a good idea for pregnant queens and young kittens. Ask your vet for advice. Always ensure that you follow the advice on the label of the packaging of supplements so that you do not overdose the cat.

Cat treats are also readily available in pet shops. If you want to give your cat treats, limit them to once or twice a week, and then do not give too many. Certain cats become overweight very easily and this must be monitored carefully. Consider the cat's treats to be part of its main meals and cut down correspondingly on the amount of food given at feeding time.

OTHER FOOD

Boiled fish such as cod or coley will make a healthy occasional treat, but this cannot form the main diet, as it will be insufficient for the cat's nutritional needs.

Finally, a word about vegetables; cats cannot digest them, although individual cats will eat them and appear to enjoy doing so. If you are a devout vegetarian, do not be tempted to extend your eating beliefs to your cat; this will do the cat no good what-soever and is extremely cruel and unnatural.

chapter
five
raising kittens

NEVER BREED MOGGIES!

This is a subject that we have touched on in previous chapters, but I feel that the message can never be stressed enough: **do not breed non-pedigree cats!** However good your intentions, you will do catdom a disservice by bringing more non-pedigrees into the world. It is a fact, albeit a very sad one, that the great majority of cats and kittens that end up in rescue shelters or as strays are non-pedigrees. Pedigree cats can also become unwanted, especially those bred by unscrupulous breeders who do not ensure that their kittens go to good homes, but there are far fewer pedigrees than moggies. Unwanted pedigree cats are often rescued and rehomed by the various breed clubs, thus eliminating the need for a rescue organisation to become involved. The main reason for pedigree cats ending up in rescue seems to be that the owners feel unable to cope with the needs of that particular breed: the extensive grooming required by a Persian, or the noisy and lively nature of the Siamese and Oriental breeds.

I believe that this predominance of non-pedigrees among unwanted cats has much to do with the cost of kittens. An 'ordinary' kitten will often be given away free or at a nominal price, whereas pedigree kittens can cost several hundred pounds. Sadly, it seems to be in many people's natures to take greater care of a belonging (even a live one) that has cost them a large sum of money than of one that cost little or nothing. This is total nonsense: a live animal has similar needs no matter how much it cost the owner

Never buy a kitten without careful consideration.

and, in an ideal world, all cats should be treated with equal respect. Unfortunately, some callous owners seem to believe that it doesn't matter if the cat runs away, dies or becomes sick, as they can always get a new one. People like these usually do not bother to vaccinate or neuter their cats, with the result that the cats spread disease and breed yet more unwanted kittens. Some people even take their cat to the nearest animal shelter when they want to go on holiday, reasoning that it will be cheaper to get a new kitten when they return than to pay for the cat to be looked after at a boarding cattery.

If moggies were rarer or as expensive as pedigrees people would be forced to think twice before acquiring one. Therefore, as long as there are too many non-pedigrees, their owners should never breed from them, even if several good homes are lined up for a planned litter. Those good homes are needed for kittens that already sit unwanted in the rescue shelters, facing death unless someone chooses them.

As a breeder of pedigrees, I am sometimes accused of contributing to the problem of unwanted cats. This is something I cannot agree with, as it is very unlikely that a person who has decided to keep a Persian cat as a pet, no doubt for its special qualities such as friendly behaviour, can be converted into giving a home to a rescued moggy instead.

Never believe the old wives' tale that female cats should be allowed to have one litter before being neutered (spayed). This is total nonsense. A female cat leads a far happier life if she is neutered without having had any kittens. She is also likely to be healthier. As for the male cat, there is a risk that he will retain certain unsocial behaviour patterns, such as spraying urine indoors, even after he has been neutered. Always have your non-pedigree cat neutered sooner rather than later, at around the age of six months.

Hamish, the author's rescued crossbreed, as a very young kitten.

If you are still not convinced that it is wrong to breed moggies, then consider the following. As a responsible person, you will want to care for your queen and her litter in the best possible way. The only way to do this properly is to raise the kittens as if they were pedigrees; otherwise you will never be completely sure that you haven't brought into the world sickly kittens that may never go on to lead normal lives. In order to breed a litter in the responsible way, you will have to undertake the following:

- Your queen must be fully grown before she has a litter so that she will be strong enough to care for her kittens. This usually means she must be at least 12 months old. Most non-pedigree queens start calling (coming into season) well before this, so you will have to lock her indoors during each call to prevent accidental matings. You will also have to put up with her very loud calling, sometimes even screaming, and possible soiling indoors, for approximately five days every three weeks. If she starts calling at the age of six months, then you can possibly look forward to a total of 40 days' worth of calling before you can have her mated.

- Your queen must be tested for the diseases Feline Leukaemia Virus (FeLV) and Feline Immunodeficiency Virus (FIV) as both are likely to be transferred via mating. You do not want your queen to pass on disease either to the tom or to her kittens, do you? Needless to say, the blood tests for these diseases can be rather costly, but I would say they are essential.

- You will have to find a tom for the mating. Like your queen, he must be blood-tested for disease, as he may otherwise pass disease to your queen and her kittens. Never be tempted to let your calling queen out to 'let nature take its course'. Any unneutered tom that roams the street is likely to carry FeLV or FIV, as well as other diseases, as he will mate indiscriminately with any calling queen. You are very unlikely to find a 'safe' tom to use for breeding, as the only

Six-week-old Benji was impossible to resist.

safe ones are those that are kept permanently confined, vaccinated and blood-tested. The only ones that usually live up to this criteria are the pedigree studs, and no pedigree stud owner is likely to let him mate with a moggy.

- You will have to make sure that your queen is perfectly healthy and that her vaccinations and wormings are up to date.
- Once your queen is confirmed pregnant, she must receive extra care and extra food. This usually means that she will need feeding four times a day as opposed to two, and she will need calcium and vitamin supplements or a special food for pregnant queens. Needless to say, she must not be allowed to go out during her pregnancy, as it would be far too dangerous for both her and her unborn kittens.
- When the kittens are due (normally between 63 to 70 days after mating) your queen must be confined to one quiet room of your house. She will need a bed, a litter tray, and food. Admittedly, non-pedigrees normally give birth very easily on their own, but problems can and do occur, such as a kitten getting stuck, or the queen failing to care for it. To prevent any disasters, you will have to be with the queen to assist if necessary when she gives birth. This means that you will not be able to leave her for more than a few minutes at a time when her time is near. You can forget about that two-hour shopping trip you had planned, or about going to work: the queen needs your support. In case she gives birth in the night, she needs to be in your bedroom or you will have to sleep in her room.
- Queens are usually very good at caring for their kittens, but you will have to assist in their weaning, which should start at around the age of four weeks. The kittens cannot be weaned on any food; you will have to invest in baby food to start with and then special kitten food. Once the kittens are about one month old, they will start using their mother's litter tray, which will mean extra work for you and yet more expense, as more cat litter will be needed. In my opinion, you should not let the queen and her kittens out; at least, not until they are fully vaccinated at 12 weeks.
- Non-pedigree kittens become independent and mature earlier than pedigree cats but, even so, they should never be sold before the age of nine weeks at the earliest. The responsible way of selling kittens is not to let them go until they have been fully vaccinated at 12 weeks.
- Once the kittens are ready to leave you will have to make as sure as possible that they are going to good, caring homes where they will be looked after properly for the rest of their natural lives. This is not as easy as it sounds.
- At the end of the day, if you have done everything properly, you will be severely out of pocket. The blood tests, the special diet for the pregnant queen, the kitten food, the extra cat litter and the vaccination of the kittens are likely to add up to several hundred pounds, especially if the litter was a large one. You will either have to accept this loss, or try to recuperate some of it by charging a high price for your kittens. Charging a high price for properly-reared kittens is certainly a responsible thing to do, but you will find that not many people are prepared to pay more than a nominal sum for a non-pedigree kitten. After all, they can always find a cheaper one elsewhere, and the fact that it may carry disease will not enter many people's minds.

Need I say more?

Tippi had to be bottle fed as a kitten, and never forgot how to do it!

KITTENS ARE OFTEN SOLD TOO YOUNG

It is a very sad fact that most non-pedigree kittens are sold far too young. Most people, out of sheer ignorance, believe that a kitten is ready to leave its mother as soon as it is weaned onto a diet of solid food. Most kittens start the weaning process at about four weeks and eat four meals of solid food a day by the age of six weeks. However, this does not mean that the kitten is fully weaned. Pedigree kittens will suckle their mother for at least ten weeks, more if the queen allows them, and moggy kittens will certainly suckle for at least eight or nine weeks. It follows that the ideal age for re-homing moggy kittens would be at nine to twelve weeks - no earlier.

Anyone who has seen eight-week-old kittens suckle their mother will realise how sickening it is to find them offered for sale at six, or even four, weeks. At this age the kitten is just not ready to be without its mother, and this premature separation will affect the kitten for the rest of its life. Sadly, hardly any non-pedigrees are sold at the correct age. As so many were unwanted in the first place, their breeders tend to want to be rid of them as soon as possible. Of the non-pedigree cats that I have kept, only one was sold at the correct age; all the others were far too young. Hamish, the Siamese/Persian crossbreed, was only two weeks old when taken from his mother. Benji, the tabby-and-white, was for sale in a pet shop as being eight weeks old. He looked younger and, when examined by a veterinary surgeon, was confirmed to be no more than six weeks.

Of course, even eight weeks would have been a touch too young. Kittens that are sold this early usually have behavioural problems when they grow up. In many cases, they still show some kitten characteristics, such as suckling, kneading with the paws and dribbling, throughout their lives. Hamish eventually developed brain damage. This was directly attributable to the extremely young age at which he was taken from his mother and the totally inadequate diet that he received. Always beware of buying a kitten that is too young. If you do, you will probably give the kitten a chance to have a good life but you will have to be prepared to spend some extra time and care on it. Quite frankly, if you didn't buy the kitten, somebody else would; the owner is unlikely to let it stay with its mother for a longer period of time simply because you refused to buy it at such an early age. However, you could try to convince the 'breeder' to let the kitten stay with its mother for a while longer by offering to pay for it in advance, and possibly also contribute towards its keep.

HOW TO RAISE YOUNG KITTENS

It is important to know how to look after a kitten that has been sold too young. A good diet is essential if the kitten is to develop properly, and a six-week-old kitten will need more frequent meals than a nine-week-old one. It will also need a milk substitute to make up for the lack of mother's milk. However, it is not enough to buy special kitten food and feed the kitten four times a day, as one would with kittens of the proper age. You will also have to spend more time with your kitten to reassure it, as it will feel lost and confused after losing its one security in life - its mother.

If your kitten is as young as four weeks (and this does happen) it will need feeding no less than six times a day. It will be old enough to take solid food, but it will still need a good supply of milk, and it may not yet have learnt how to lap milk from a saucer or cope with solid food. Your first task will be to find out what the kitten can do. If it shows that it knows how to lap milk and eat solid food, then all is straightforward. Buy a good milk substitute for puppies and kittens (preferably one manufactured specially for kittens) and make sure that the kitten always has free access to this. Do not forget to change the milk regularly, as it will probably start to deteriorate after a few hours. Most good pet shops will sell this type of milk substitute, as will many vets. Carefully follow the instructions on the packaging for mixing the milk. Too strong a mixture will mean that the kitten will probably suffer from an upset stomach and too weak a mixture will mean that it will not receive all the nutrients that it still needs.

As well as milk, the kitten will need a meal of solid food six times a day. Many special kitten diets are available from pet shops and also from some vets. For a kitten as young as four weeks you should choose canned food rather than dry, as this will be easier for the kitten to chew and digest at such a tender age. Alternatively, you could buy a good-quality dry kitten food and soak it in the milk substitute until it is thoroughly soft. Never give a kitten cow's milk, as this is likely to cause severe stomach upsets.

If the kitten is not yet able to lap milk and eat solid food you will have to wean it. A four-week-old kitten should be able to feed itself, so that you do not have to resort to bottle feeding.

The way to get a kitten to lap milk is to stick your finger into the milk, gently putting this into the kitten's mouth and also around the mouth to show the kitten what it is. It may take time, perhaps several attempts a day for a few days, but eventually the kitten will realise what is expected of it and start to lap. If it takes more than a day to teach the kitten to lap you will have to bottle-feed it in the meantime.

The process of teaching a kitten to eat solid food is very much the same. The first food that you introduce should be very sloppy and not really solid at all. Your best option here is to use baby-food intended for the youngest of babies, often referred to as Stage One food, of a suitable flavour, such as chicken, lamb or fish. Avoid baby-food that contains a large proportion of vegetables, as the kitten is less likely to accept this. Mix some of the kitten milk with the baby-food and again use the 'finger' method. Once the kitten has started to lap this sloppy mixture you can feed it without mixing in any milk. As soon as the kitten is eating this confidently, try changing it for special kitten food. Normally, this whole process only takes two or three days - occasionally as long as a week.

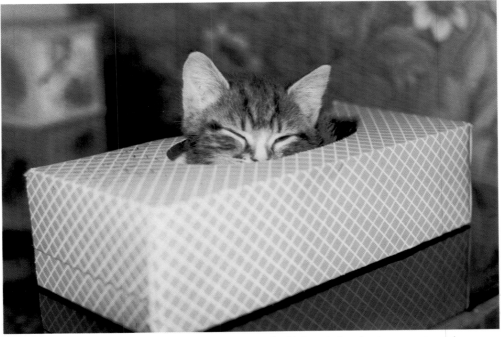

Six-week-old Tippi's first bed was a tissue box.

If your kitten is five to six weeks old the number of meals given each day should not be less than five. Otherwise, you should follow the same procedure, although most kittens of this age know how to lap milk and eat solid food.

From the age of seven weeks, four meals a day will be sufficient, but an unlimited supply of milk should still be available. It is best to let any kitten taken too young from its mother have a milk substitute to drink until it is approximately four months old, and four meals a day should be given for a minimum of four months. At five months three meals a day will be enough and, once the kitten reaches maturity at nine months, two meals will suffice.

A kitten separated too early from its mother will also need extra support from you, its new 'mother'. For security, it may want to sleep next to you in bed or, if you object, in a cat bed or cardboard box with a hot water bottle. An old trick is to cover a ticking

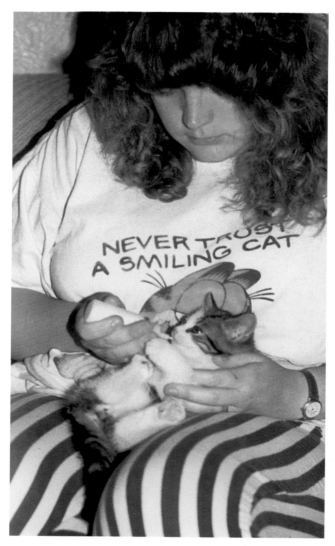

Some kittens are sold too young and must be bottle fed.

clock up with a blanket in the kitten's bed, as this will remind it of its mother's heartbeat. Some kittens are so upset at having lost their mother that they insist on suckling. They may try to suckle your ears, your hair - anything. In the case of a kitten like this, it may be an idea to give the occasional bottled meal to make it feel more secure.

HAND-REARING ORPHANED KITTENS

You may suddenly find yourself the owner of motherless kittens less than four weeks old, perhaps even newborn. People do cruel things, and it isn't all that unusual to find abandoned newborn kittens discarded as rubbish. Perhaps an outdoor queen with kittens has been killed in a road accident or similar; her kittens will then need to be reared. It is very hard work to hand-rear a whole litter of orphaned kittens, but it is also very rewarding. If you do take on this task, it is vital for the kittens' well-being that you know how to go about it properly.

The first thing to sort out is suitable accommodation for the kitten or kittens. Very young kittens are not yet able to regulate their body temperatures, so it is vital that they are kept in an environment that is neither too cold nor too hot. Newborn to two-week-old kittens need to be kept at a constant temperature of around 30-34°C, which is far higher than will be found in most homes, even in the summer. You will need to place the kittens in a box or cat bed (not too big, but big enough for the kittens to move around once their eyes are open) with some soft, dry bedding. Veterinary bedding is ideal, as this will allow dampness to seep through to the bottom of the bed while the surface stays dry. It is very important that the kittens are not kept in damp or draughty conditions. Under the box or bed you can place a heated pad. Avoid putting this inside the bed in case it gets damp. Leave a thermometer inside the bed for a while to make sure you have the temperature about right. Alternatively, a hot-water-bottle can be used, although care must then be taken to ensure that it does not get too cold and that it is not too hot when first placed in the bed.

For the third week of life, kittens should be kept at a temperature of around 30°C, which will then be lowered to 25°C during the fourth week. Once the kittens are five weeks old they can safely be kept at 20°C which is only just above normal room temperature. If it is winter, or if you live in a particularly cold house, you may want to put extra bedding into the kittens' bed to keep them warm. The heated pad should not be necessary by now, and you will also probably find that kittens of this age will gradually start to sleep wherever they choose, which more often than not is not the bed or box they were originally kept in.

So far we have assumed that the kitten or kittens you are hand-rearing are normal, healthy ones, with no additional problems. In the case of very weak or sickly kittens, or kittens with deformities, it can be very difficult for the novice to attempt hand-rearing. If you are doubtful about the kittens' health, always consult your vet.

From birth until the age of two weeks, orphaned kittens will need feeding every two hours, day and night. Miss one feed and you may have a dying kitten on your hands. It is extremely important to feed the kittens regularly, as this is their only chance of survival. If you are not sure how old your kittens are, the eyes are normally a good guide. Most kittens open their eyes at the age of six to twelve days. Any kitten whose eyes are still closed or just starting to show as small slits is certainly under the age of two weeks and should be treated as newborn. A kitten's ears do not open until it is

A well-cared-for kitten has the best chance of a healthy life.

14 days old, so this can also be used as a guide. The teeth do not come through until three or four weeks.

Once the kittens are two weeks old you can gradually lower the number of feeds given, simultaneously increasing the amount given at each feed. The best way to do this is to increase the intervals between each feed and eventually drop the nightly feeds, giving you a chance of some well-earned rest! A good guide is to give nine feeds daily from the age of two weeks, spread evenly over day and night. From three weeks you should be able to drop the night feeds, as long as the kittens are fed at around midnight, and then first thing in the morning, six or seven hours later. They now need seven meals a day. As mentioned earlier, six meals will be needed at four weeks, five at five weeks, and from seven to eight weeks onwards four is sufficient. The amount should be around 2ml per feed for newborn kittens, which should then gradually be increased as the kitten grows. Each kitten should be allowed to take as much milk as it wants per feed.

It is best to feed a kitten with a special kitten feeding bottle, which you can purchase from a pet shop. Follow the manufacturer's instructions carefully. It is very important that the hole in the teat is of the correct size, so that small drops will just drip out when the bottle is held upside down. If the hole is too large, the kitten will feed too quickly, and may end up actually inhaling milk, with pneumonia as a direct result. Similarly, a teat with too small a hole is wrong, as the kitten will not be able to take enough milk. It can be very difficult to pierce the teat for the feeding bottle accurately. One way is to use a small pair of scissors (sterilised by boiling) and gently snip a small hole in the teat. A large needle, sterilised either by boiling or by being held inside a naked flame for a few moments, can also be used.

An alternative to the feeding bottle is a syringe without the needle. This has the advantage of showing you exactly how much milk the kitten has taken. The disadvantage is that very young kittens cannot suck naturally from a syringe, so you will have to help them by depressing the syringe gently to make the milk appear. If this is not done very carefully the kitten may get too much too quickly, with dire consequences. If milk starts bubbling out of the kitten's nostrils you know that the milk is flowing too fast. This may also happen with kittens born with deformities such as cleft palates. Any such kitten will not usually be able to take much milk at all, so is best put to sleep.

Always remember to keep the feeding equipment sterilised, either by boiling or by using sterilising tablets like those used for babies' bottles. Follow the instructions carefully, or the kitten may get a stomach upset caused by bacteria.

Any brand of milk that can be bought from pet shops and vets is suitable, but preferably one intended specifically for kittens, rather than one for kittens and puppies. Always follow the manufacturers' instructions carefully. If you cannot obtain a suitable milk substitute you can make your own. Mix 1.6ml (5 fl oz) of evaporated milk together with the same amount of cooled, boiled water, not water straight from the tap. Then add one small egg yolk (no white) and one level teaspoon of glucose. Always make sure that each feed is freshly made up unless you keep it refrigerated (but not for longer than 24 hours) and gently heat up the right amount for each feed. Milk should be given at body temperature; colder and warmer can both cause problems for the kittens. Never re-heat milk that has already been heated once.

Once the kittens are four weeks old you should start to introduce some solid food into their diet, as described earlier.

As orphan kittens will not have a mother to lick them, you will have to be a substitute here as well. Bottle-fed kittens can get very dirty and their skin will also need rubbing to ensure proper blood circulation. Gently wipe the kitten with a damp cloth after each feed. Kittens younger than three weeks will need to be stimulated to defecate and urinate. The best method is to wipe the kitten's nether region with a damp, warm flannel or piece of cotton wool, imitating the mother licking the kittens.

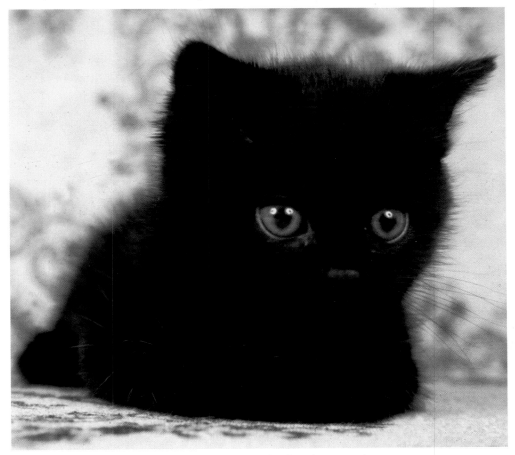

Don't be fooled by cute pictures. Kittens need a lot of care and attention.

SEXING KITTENS

A word on sexing kittens: this is best done at birth or a few days afterwards, before too much fur is covering the evidence! Basically, the distance between the genitalia and the anus is much greater in the male than the female. If you have two kittens of different sexes to compare, you will be able to sex them easily. The male also has a slightly 'puffed-up' appearance around his genitalia.

chapter *six*

showing non-pedigree cats

Showing non-pedigrees? Surely cat shows are for pedigrees only?

Many people believe this, but nothing could be further from the truth. It is quite possible to show your ordinary, fireside cat at a championship cat show, and many people do. At the largest cat shows it is possible to find a hundred or more moggies and cross-bred cats shown in the non-pedigree section, also referred to as the household pet section. Showing cats can become a very fulfilling hobby and every owner of a non-pedigree has as good a chance of winning no matter what their cat looks like, as long as it is in good condition, has a good temperament and enjoys being shown. All sorts of people, of all ages, show non-pedigree cats, even pedigree breeders. There are often special classes for cats owned by children and by senior citizens, and nobody needs to feel left out. In fact, many people have started by showing non-pedigree cats, only to go on to showing pedigrees later as their interest grew.

In Britain, the largest organisation that licenses shows is also the oldest: the Governing Council of the Cat Fancy (GCCF). The GCCF itself only organises one show every year, the Supreme Cat Show, but it grants licenses to many of its affiliated clubs to hold shows under the GCCF's rules. There are about 120 GCCF-licensed shows every year and the great majority of these have household pet sections. There are other societies in Britain, unaffiliated to the GCCF, that hold cat shows. These are very much the minority, so this chapter deals mainly with

GCCF-style shows, as these are the ones most people are likely to encounter. The non-GCCF organisations and their policies on non-pedigree showing are discussed, however, and there is also a section on showing household pets in the USA.

THE NON-PEDIGREE SHOW CAT

What constitutes a non-pedigree cat? Non-pedigree (household pet) cats are described within the GCCF as: '... unregistered cats of unregistered/unknown parent or parents' and no registered cat may be exhibited in classes offered for them. This means any ordinary moggy, any cross-bred cat or any rescued pedigree cat of unknown pedigree. Almost all non-pedigree

Any friendly, well-tended non-pedigree cat can become a show winner.

show cats are rescued moggies and cross-breeds. Cross-breeds, often referred to as 'half pedigrees', are cats that, for example, have one pedigree parent and one moggy parent. 'Rescued' can mean cats that have been adopted as strays or re-homed through an animal shelter, cat club or similar organisation.

I think the non-pedigree show cat should be a rescued cat. Any cat that has been deliberately bred for showing is very much frowned upon by the exhibitors of rescued non-pedigrees; non-pedigrees should not be bred deliberately, as there are already so many in desperate need of good homes. Unfortunately, the GCCF rules regarding what constitutes a non-pedigree cat are vague and open to abuse. At the moment there are moves for having these rules tightened or changed, so things may be different in the future.

Some people breed kittens from unregistered pedigree parents and then, quite in

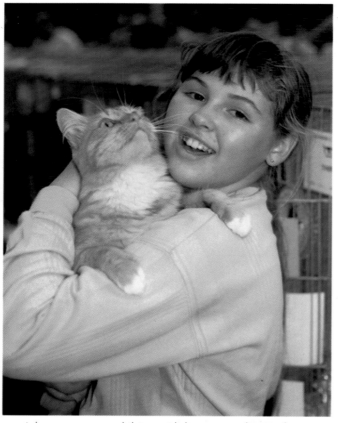

A happy young exhibitor with her non-pedigree show cat.

accordance with the rules, show the kittens as non-pedigrees as they fulfil the criterion of being bred from unregistered parents. It is not possible to show a pedigree cat, even if it is unregistered, if both its parents are known and registered. On the other hand, it is possible to show a rescued pedigree cat, as its owner genuinely does not have access to its pedigree papers, and does not know who the cat's parents are. These cats are normally shown in classes such as 'half-pedigree' or 'any cat of obvious pedigree type but with unknown parents'.

What should be borne in mind is that a cat that has been deliberately bred by a caring owner has a much better start in life than the majority of rescued cats, which often have been taken from their mothers too early, abandoned or mis-treated. It has learned from an early age to trust people, including strangers, and has always been in good condition. The show-winning non-pedigree cat that really deserves to be admired is one that, having been rescued from a life of misery, has been so well tended by its new owner that it is now in sparkling condition and has learned to trust even strangers. (Read more about cats like this in Chapter 9.)

The show non-pedigree cat is judged only according to its condition and tempera-ment. Looks should not really matter at all apart from when a judge is faced with several equally good cats and has to choose a winner. In such a case, the judge will probably go for personal preference and pick the cat whose colour appeals the most. However, this is not a very common occurrence, as usually it is quite possible to pick the winner from condition and temperament only.

So, what do good condition and temperament actually mean? Some novice exhibitors seem to think that it means simply that the cat is not ill and behaves well at home. The truth is that a good non-pedigree show cat needs much more than this. First of all, not all moggies make good show cats. A cat that behaves perfectly well at home can undergo a sudden character change when faced with being penned at a show and handled by several strangers. It may either turn into a snarling tiger that will not let anyone near, or become a nervous wreck that hides under its blanket all day. Needless to say, if your cat exhibits any of these tendencies, it should never be shown again. The cat **must** enjoy itself; otherwise the whole exercise is pointless. No caring cat owner wants to put his or her cat through a stressful, unenjoyable situation, and a cat that is not relaxed at a show stands little or no chance of winning. The show non-pedigree cat will relax at a show, enjoying the experience of being cuddled and admired by many people. It is usually outgoing and friendly, purring and rubbing up against the hands of the judges. Some cats that are very trusting and friendly while in the pen get rather worried when picked up or placed on the judge's table. Most judges are tolerant towards this and the cat can still get a good placing although, if there is another cat that is equally good and doesn't mind any kind of handling, then naturally the latter will win.

However, a good temperament alone is not enough for a non-pedigree cat to win. The cat must be in general good condition (neither too fat nor too thin) and it must have been well prepared for the show. A dirty or badly-groomed cat will not be placed, no matter how friendly and healthy it is.

All non-pedigree cats, shorthaired and longhaired, will benefit from a bath before the show. A shorthaired cat should be bathed several days in advance, perhaps as early as one week (providing it has no opportunity to get dirty again), as its coat needs this long to recover some of the natural oils that a shampooing removes. Without these, the coat neither shines nor lays flat. A longhaired cat should be bathed two or three days before the show. Again, if the bath is given too close to the show the coat will lack lustre and not look its best.

All cats need a good grooming session before the show, a shorthaired cat with a fine-toothed metal comb or a brush and a longhaired cat with a medium- and fine-toothed comb. In the case of longhairs, it is very important to make sure that the coat is completely tangle-free.

A non-pedigree cat intended for showing should not wear a collar. All collars tend to mark the fur, making it thinner around the cat's neck, and this may go against your cat as it will spoil the overall appearance.

Make sure that the cat's eyes and ears are perfectly clean. If they are not, the cat will not even be let into the show hall. Trim the claws a couple of days before the show. Just snip the very tips off, to prevent the cat from scratching the judge accidentally. Many judges check whether the claws have been trimmed.

The cat's teeth should be clean and in good condition, and that means free of tartar. The gums should look healthy and must not be inflamed. This is something that many people tend to forget about and it can be very disappointing for a judge to find a lovely cat that appears to be in tip-top condition, only to discover that its mouth does not come up to standard. Every little detail matters when showing non-pedigrees; often competition is hard and the aim is, after all, to find the friendliest, best-presented cat. A non-pedigree cat that is shown regularly and enjoys the experience is not an animal to be pitied, as many people seem to think. Even some rescue groups hold the opinion that showing cats is cruel. If anything, a seasoned show non-pedigree cat is better looked after and in better condition than the average pet cat, simply because it stands no chance of winning unless its condition is absolutely top. Few cats get checked over by vets as regularly as show cats, as no cat is allowed inside the show hall without first being examined by one of the show vets.

ENTERING A SHOW

Entering a cat show is not simply a case of turning up with your non-pedigree cat on the day. Entries usually have to be made around six weeks in advance of the show. Details of shows can be found in the various cat magazines, especially the GCCF's official weekly journal *Cats*. If you want to be sure you do not miss the advertisement for any particular show you can order a list of all GCCF-licensed shows (covering 12 months from 1 June to 31 May) from the GCCF for a small fee. The list tells you whether a particular show is a championship show, a sanction show or an exemption show. All clubs wishing to stage shows have to work their way up from exemption show through sanction shows until eventually they may be granted championship status. For the non-pedigree exhibitor either type of show does just as well, as the difference between the three types mainly concerns pedigree cats:

- A **championship show** is a full scale show where Challenge Certificates (CCs) are on offer for pedigree cats. These are the certificates that pedigree cats collect to attain the title 'Champion'. There are a great number of classes and, for the non-pedigree cats, there is the prestigious Whiskas class (see pages 76-77). A championship show can be an all-breed show with an entry that can be of over 1000 cats, representing all different breeds as well as non-pedigrees. It can cover just a group of breeds, such as Longhairs, or just one breed, such as Siamese. Most championship shows offer classes for non-pedigree cats, and this is indicated in the various advertisements as 'with Household Pet Section', or simply by the letter 'HP'. (This is the same for all types of show.)
- A **sanction show** is basically the same as a championship show only without the certificates and the Whiskas classes. It could be called a 'dress rehearsal' for a championship show, as this is the intention.
- An **exemption show** is a small show which is exempt from certain GCCF rules. The entries are often around the 100 mark and fewer classes are on offer. This type of show can be an excellent start for the novice exhibitor who feels a bit apprehensive at the prospect of a large championship show.

Once you have decided which show you want to enter, write to the Show Manager or Assistant Show Manager (the person to contact is listed in the advertisement) and request a schedule. Do not forget to include a stamped addressed envelope. Some clubs send show schedules to all their members automatically, others post schedules to anyone who exhibited at their last show, but normally you have to write in for one. Do this well in advance. Schedules are usually available about three months before the date of the show.

You will find the non-pedigree classes listed at the back of the show schedule. Every cat must be entered into the appropriate open class before being entered into any other classes. The open class, best described as the 'breed class', is the most important class at the show. The number and description of open classes vary from show to show. Read the class names, and select the one that best suits your cat. It should only be possible to enter your cat into one open class.

The open classes for non-pedigree cats are based on the cats' colouring, fur length and, sometimes, age. However, the classes vary considerably, the number depending on how many entries this particular show is expecting. A large show may have one class for every common colour, or perhaps even two: one for shorthairs and one for longhairs. A smaller show may group several colours together, such as 'any colour self' or 'any longhair'. Large shows usually have both an adult and a kitten class for each colour or group of colours, but small shows may have only one or two classes specifically for kittens. All shows usually have an Any Other Colour (AOC) class so, if your cat is an unusual colour that doesn't fit into any of the other listed open classes, this is the class for you. Most shows also have one class for 'half-pedigree cats' - normally cats bred from one pedigree and one moggy parent, or a class along the line of 'any cat obviously of pedigree type but with unknown parentage'.

Darroby Gizmo, BIS at the Lord Mayor's Show, Hull 1992.
Owned and photographed by E Wardle.

If you are still unsure which class to enter you can telephone the Section Manager for help and advice. The larger championship shows usually have one person dealing exclusively with non-pedigree entries. The smaller shows may have two or three people

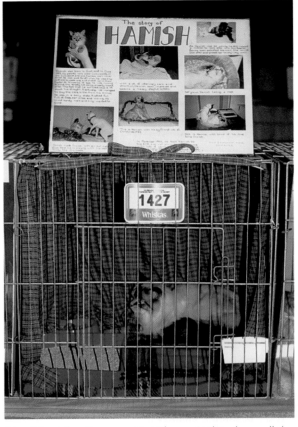

dealing with the various breed sections between them.

For the purpose of showing at GCCF shows, a kitten is a cat of no less than 14 weeks of age, but under nine months. If you do not know your cat's exact date of birth you will have to estimate or ask a vet for help. An adult cat is aged nine months and over. A very important rule is that all adult non-pedigree cats must be neutered. An adult unneutered non-pedigree cat will be disqualified.

Once you have selected the appropriate open class for your cat, it is time to have a look at the list of side classes. These are extra classes, mainly added for fun, but they are well worth entering as they increase your cat's chances of winning. Even if your cat has not been placed in its open

Hamish at the Supreme Cat Show. At this show all the pens are decorated.

class it may still win in one of its side classes. Every cat must be entered into a minimum of four classes: one open and three side. Most shows offer the opportunity to enter into more than three side classes, for an extra fee. (The four compulsory classes are all included in the entry fee.) Details of classes are always listed in the show schedule so you should read it carefully.

The side classes can be almost any type of class. For non-pedigree cats, typical side classes are: 'Any cat owned by a person under 16', 'Any rescued cat', 'Senior cat' (over two years), 'Veteran cat' (over seven years), 'Most unusual colour', 'Best groomed cat', 'Prettiest female', 'Biggest eyes' and 'Longest whiskers'. In other words, they could be anything - that's the fun with them!

The final type of class, only found at championship shows, is the Whiskas class. This is purely for non-pedigree cats and adds some extra competition and excitement to the household pet section. These classes, sponsored by the manufacturers of Whiskas cat food, are always very well supported, and it could be argued that they are the most important classes in any household pet section. There are always five Whiskas classes at each championship show:

- Longhair non-self.
- Longhair or shorthair self.
- Shorthair tabby or tabby-and-white.
- Shorthair ginger, ginger-and-white, tortie or tortie-and-white.
- Shorthair any other colour non-self.

All classes are open to both kittens and adults. The first three cats placed in each class receive a cat food voucher and a rosette, fourth and fifth placed cats receive a rosette. Once all the winners have been selected, all five compete for the Overall Best Whiskas Cat. The winner receives more vouchers, a large rosette, and qualifies for entry to the prestigious Whiskas Finals, held at the Supreme Cat Show. Once a cat has qualified for the final by winning Best Overall Whiskas, it may not compete in any further heats of the competition until the Supreme Cat Show. At the Supreme show, the same five classes are available for all the qualifying cats to compete for the top spot, the Whiskas Champion. The winner receives many prizes, such as a crystal trophy and a year's supply of Whiskas cat food, and the four runners-up are well rewarded also.

Once you have selected the open class, the side classes and the Whiskas class it is time to fill in the entry form. Most cat clubs supply a separate entry form for non-pedigree cats which is much simpler than the one provided for pedigrees. However, some clubs expect you to use the same form as for pedigree cats, in which case it is important to know which details must be included. Read the schedule carefully; it should state exactly what details non-pedigree cat exhibitors are required to give. Normally, any non-pedigree exhibitor has to list the cat's **Name, Age** (or approximate date of birth), **Sex** (which should read **M** for male and **F** for female, **MN** for male neuter and **FN** for female neuter), whether the cat is **Shorthaired (SH)** or **Longhaired (LH)**, the **Colour** of the cat, and which **Classes** you want it entered into, as well as your name, address and telephone number. (Your telephone number is for the Section Manager's use only, in case you need to be contacted - it is not published in the show catalogue.)

You also have to sign an agreement saying that you will abide by the GCCF's show rules. A summary of these rules is printed on the entry form, but if you want to read the whole section you can order it from the GCCF for a small fee. One important rule is that every cat entered must have been vaccinated not more than 12 months and usually not less than 7 to 14 days before the show. None of your cats (even those not attending the show) must suffer from any infectious diseases. Finally, you must abide by what is known as the **13-day rule**. This rule states that nobody can show more frequently than every other week and there must be a gap of at least 13 days between each show that you enter. This is regardless of whether you enter the same cat or two different cats in two consecutive shows. The object is to prevent the spread of disease, and the rule must be respected. It also prevents people from 'over-showing' their cats, as it ensures that each cat has a rest of at least 13 days between each show. Failure to comply with this rule results in disciplinary action from the GCCF.

Once you have filled in your entry form, check it over again to make sure that you have filled it in correctly and have not forgotten to include any important information. Then photocopy the form before sending it off, keeping the copy for your own reference. This is important as proof of what you actually wrote on the entry form and also a good way of jogging your memory; it is so easy to forget which classes you entered when you filled in the form two or three months before the show. Send the entry form and the entry fee to the Household Pet Section Manager. You also want to enclose a stamped addressed postcard for acknowledgement of your entry. Then check the schedule again, regarding **tallies**. These are the little number tags that exhibitors have to tie around their cats' necks at the show. Some shows post these to all exhibitors a week or so before the show, in which case you also need to enclose a stamped addressed envelope. Other organisers hand them out at the show.

The final point on the subject of entering shows is **timing**. Most cat shows are very well supported and each has a set limit for how many cats they can accept. Show Managers sometimes have to return entries simply because the set number of exhibits has been reached. For this reason you should enter your cat as soon as possible. Do not leave it to the last few days before the entries close or you may be in for disappointment. Entries are accepted on a 'first come, first served' basis.

THE SUPREME CAT SHOW

The Supreme deserves a special mention as it is the only GCCF show that differs to any degree from the others. The Supreme is the GCCF's own show. It has often been referred to as 'the Crufts of the Cat Fancy' and, in many ways, it is very similar to that famous dog show. The Supreme is held once a year and it is a large show, usually with around 1200 exhibits. The non-pedigree section typically attracts an entry of over 100. It is the most prestigious cat show in Great Britain, and the only one where each and every cat entered must first have qualified for entry by winning at another show. Needless to say, with so many winning cats under one roof, the quality of every cat is extremely high, competition is fierce but friendly, and excitement is high all day. A non-pedigree cat qualifies for entry into the Supreme Cat Show by winning a first prize in its open class at any championship show. A first prize in any Whiskas class qualifies for entry into the Supreme classes. However, to qualify for the Whiskas Finals your cat must previously have been an overall Whiskas winner.

At the Supreme, you can only enter one class with your cat unless it has qualified for the Whiskas finals, in which case you enter the appropriate Whiskas class as well. The Supreme also differs from other shows in the actual judging. Each cat is judged in a judging ring, at a table where the judge is seated. Stewards carry the cats in their own carriers to the judging table. Usually an entire class is brought in at any one time, and the cats are penned around the table in the usual type of show pens, furnished only with white blankets. Thus the judge does not know which cat belongs to which exhibitor. Each cat receives a written critique, stating the cat's placing in the class and the judge's comments. The critique is attached to the cat's pen after the cat has been judged.

As no cat is judged at its own pen, owners are encouraged to decorate their pens. The pens are twice the normal size at 120cm x 60cm (4ft x 2ft) and owners come up with the most ingenious designs. There are competitions for the best decorated, such as 'The most amusing pen' or 'The most original pen', so everybody joins in as imaginatively as possible. Non-pedigree cats entered into the Whiskas finals are judged at their pens but, as long as no reference is made on the pen to the cat's name, these may still be decorated. The main judging then takes place in the judging ring.

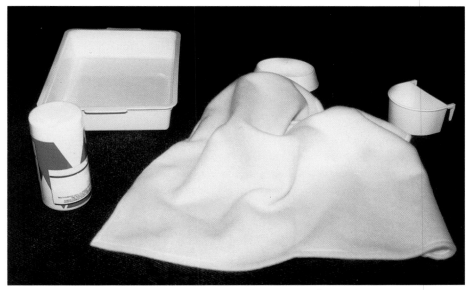

Show equipment: white litter tray, bowls and blanket together with cage wipes.

Other than this, cats are judged in the normal way, under the same criteria. As the day progresses, winners are selected, until finally there is one Best Shorthair, one Best Longhair and the five Whiskas winners. The Whiskas winners is judged on stage (and the judging can be watched on TV monitors all over the hall) and the Whiskas Champion is selected. Then the Best Shorthair Non-pedigree and the Best Longhair Non-pedigree compete against each other on the stage and the Supreme Household Pet is chosen.

PREPARING FOR A SHOW

Most of the necessary show preparations, such as bathing your cat, trimming its claws, and ensuring that its ears are free of wax, have already been mentioned. You also need to pack all that you need for the show day. For your cat you need:

- Thin white ribbon or elastic to tie the cat's number tally around its neck.
- A small, white litter tray. The cat's pen must be furnished in white only, with no distinguishing marks.
- Cat litter for the tray. This can usually be bought at the show but you ought to bring some, just to be on the safe side.
- A white show blanket, suitable for a pen of the standard size 60cm x 60cm (2ft x 2ft). This blanket must be plain and not of the cellular type. Special show blankets can be bought at most shows. An alternative to this is absorbent veterinary bedding, which is white with green backing.
- Two white bowls (plastic), one for water and one for food.
- Food for your cat.
- A good-quality cat-carrier to transport your cat to the show.
- Comb and/or brush to groom your cat prior to judging. This is especially important if your cat is longhaired.

Other than this you should bring your cat's Vaccination Certificate and your show schedule. Other useful items may be a book to read, some tissue in case your cat has an 'accident' in its carrier, money for a show catalogue (unless you paid for one in advance with your entry) and to get yourself something to eat. Some people bring a mild disinfectant so that they can wipe their cat's pen to minimise the risk of infection, but it must be stressed that the risk is extremely small.

THE SHOW DAY

The show day probably means an early start for you and your cat. The times for vetting-in and judging are given in your schedule, so check these carefully. Normally, you are expected to arrive at the show between 8.00am and 9.45am, as judging starts at around 10.00am. Don't leave yourself too little time at the show hall. Preparing your pen and your cat (especially if it needs grooming) may take up to half an hour, and you do not want to rush.

Before you set off for the show, give your cat a final going over. Check that it is as clean as possible, that you have not forgotten to trim the claws and, most importantly, that there are no fleas. It is probably best not to feed your cat before you leave, as you never know whether the journey will upset its stomach. You can always feed your cat when you arrive at the show. Place a comfortable blanket in your cat's carrier (which must be a proper transporter as cardboard ones are not accepted) but do not use the

Right: Judging at a GCCF-style show.
Above: A striking red-tabby-and-white cat being judged.

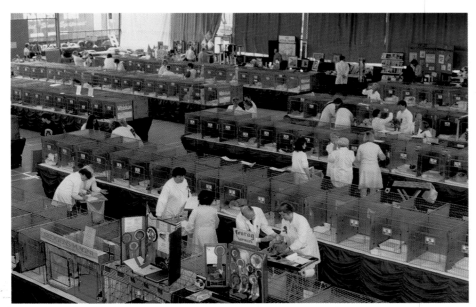

white blanket that you need for the show. If your cat has an unfortunate 'accident' whilst in its travelling box, you don't want to find yourself without a clean show blanket.

On arrival at the show hall, follow the signs for the vetting-in queue. First, you will need to stop at the checking-in table, where you give your name and receive an envelope containing the cat's tally, the vetting-in card, your exhibitor's ticket and anything else you may have requested. If these items have been sent to you in advance normally you only have to give your name, so that the organisers can tick you off their list. If you have entered more than one cat but for one reason or another have not brought them all, now is the time to tell the organisers.

Once you have collected your exhibitor's envelope, find the vetting-in card and keep it to hand. This card lists your name and address, all your cat's details, and the pen number allocated to you. No exhibitor is allowed into the show unless one of the officiating vets has signed this card, certifying that your cat has been examined and found to be healthy.

Your next stop is the vetting-in. A number of vets will be officiating, and you wait your turn and then go to the table pointed out to you. Hand your vetting-in card to the vet or the steward and remove your cat from its carrier. The vet checks that the cat is healthy and fit to be exhibited. This includes checking the eyes, nose and ears for discharge, the mouth for any signs of illness, the tail area, which must be clean, and the coat and skin, which should be clean and unbroken. The vets are instructed to be as thorough as possible and only cats in perfect health are let through. A cat with a sore eye will probably be rejected, as will one with any signs of fleas (even if it is only flea dirt), dirty ears, or the tiniest mark on its skin in case this should turn out to be ringworm, even if you know full well that your cat received it whilst playing with another cat. The vetting-in procedure is quite nerve-wracking and even the most seasoned exhibitor worries that the vet will find something wrong.

If your cat is rejected for any reason you will be escorted to the isolation room, where the cat must spend the day unless you live near enough to the exhibition hall to return home. If your cat is deemed to be suffering from something contagious neither you nor your cat will be allowed to enter the show hall. You will be given a rejection slip signed by the vet, stating why your cat was rejected. There are several categories under which a cat can be rejected at the show, and what you should do next depends on why your cat was rejected. Sometimes you will not be required to do anything, but under certain circumstances you may be banned from showing until the GCCF has received a certificate from your vet stating that all your cats are healthy.

All this may seem very daunting, but it has to be understood that the whole procedure of vetting-in is to protect the cats; no cat suffering from a contagious disease should be allowed inside the show hall. In describing the vetting-in procedure, I have also tried to underline exactly why it is so important to bring a clean, healthy cat to the show. It is not simply that the cat in the best condition may win, and that a cat in poor condition will lose; the cat in poor condition may never even reach its show pen!

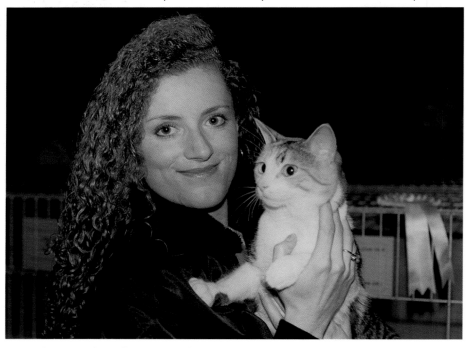

A cat show can be a fun day out for cat and owner alike.

Once your vetting-in card has been signed you can enter the hall and find your cat's pen. You need to furnish the pen before settling in your cat. Place the blanket in the pen, spreading it over the entire pen if it is a normal or cold day but perhaps leaving it folded in half if it is warm, as most cats prefer to sit away from the blanket if it is hot. If your cat cannot avoid the blanket, the likelihood is that it will choose its litter tray to rest in. Put litter in the litter tray and place it at one side of the pen. Fill the water bowl (normally the type that you hook onto the bars of the pen) and place it at the back, in

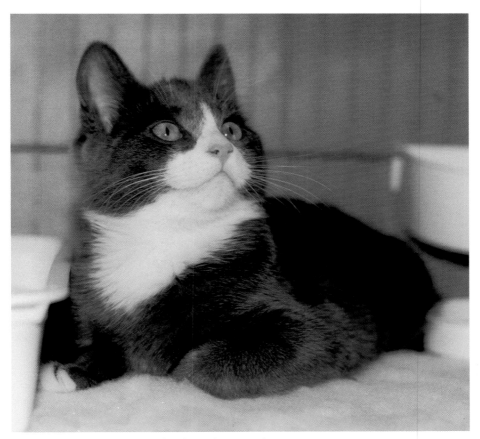

A non-pedigree cat waiting for the judge at a show.

accordance with the show rules. You can feed your cat now, but the food bowl must be removed when judging is about to start. You can put it back later. I prefer to give my cat dry food at a show, as canned food may smear around its mouth or chest, especially on a longhaired animal.

Get your cat out and give it a final grooming. After this, place the tally around its neck with the white ribbon or elastic. Now you are finished.

Talk to your cat to see how it settles in. Some cats may be calmer if they are left alone, trying to get out of the pen as soon as they see their owners but settling down for a rest when they are out of sight. If this is the case, leave the cat and take the opportunity to have a look around.

An announcement will be made when judging is about to commence and all exhibitors then have to leave the hall. Now is the time to buy your show catalogue and check that your cat's details have been entered correctly. If there is any mistake, such as your cat being placed in the wrong class, you have to inform the Household Pet Section Manager immediately so that this can be rectified. Each Section Manager has his or her own table clearly labelled.

You can watch the judging from outside the pen area. Each judge moves from pen to pen accompanied by a steward pushing a trolley. As the judge stops by a pen the steward takes out the cat and places it on the trolley for the judge's inspection. When this exhibit has been judged the steward replaces it in its pen. Trolley and hands are then disinfected before the next exhibit is judged.

From your catalogue, you can see what competition your cat is up against in terms of the size of classes. This is one of the most exciting parts of the day: the smaller the class, the greater your cat's chance of being placed. In fact, if your cat is the single entry in a class you are almost certain of a first! Non-pedigree judges are very lenient, realising that all the exhibits are people's beloved pets, so seldom withhold awards unless the cat is particularly bad-tempered.

During the judging you have an excellent opportunity to have something to eat, talk to other exhibitors, read a book or visit the trade stands. It is only while the open classes are being judged that exhibitors are not allowed into the hall, and this usually takes two-and-a-half to three hours. When all the open classes have been judged (and possibly some of the side classes as well) the judges break for lunch and all exhibitors and visitors to the show are let into the hall.

Rescued cat Kit Carson, owned by Linda Jones, has had a very successful show career, winning BIS Kitten at his first show and having had many BIS wins since.

While you are waiting, you can check the award boards to see how your cat is doing. Look for the number of its open class and see if there is a completed judging slip yet. If there is, First, Second, Third and possibly Fourth will be listed, preceded by the pen number of the winning cat. Do not be too disappointed if your cat has not won. Unless your cat really does not like showing, you may well find yourself the owner of the winner at the next show. Even if you do not, remember that the cat you brought to the show is the pet you love, and shows should be fun.

Normally cats are placed from first to third in each class, occasionally first to fourth. The prizes are usually rosettes. Some shows offer prize money but the sums involved are very small. Other shows give out both prize cards and rosettes, while some of the smaller ones only offer prize cards, with rosettes for the main winners. Most shows select an overall Best In Show (BIS) Household Pet and this cat is selected from the winners of all the open classes. Similarly, all shows with Whiskas classes on offer select an overall Whiskas Winner. The Best In Show (BIS) and the Whiskas Winner may be the same cat, but they are often two different cats, so there are two chances to have a top winner.

Most shows close at 5.00 pm and you cannot leave earlier unless you have been granted special permission by the Show Manager. Sometimes a show may close early; if this is the case it will be announced over the loudspeakers.

That's it; your very first show is over! Both you and your cat will probably be rather tired by now but, whether you arrive back home with or without a collection of rosettes, you both should have had an enjoyable day. If so, the chances are that you will soon start planning for the next show...

THE CAT ASSOCIATION OF BRITAIN (CA)

The Cat Association of Britain is another governing body in this country that registers cats and holds shows. The CA is the British member of FIFe (Fédération Internationale Féline), the international governing body for the cat fancy. Most governing bodies in Europe are FIFe members, and they all have to adhere to the same show rules and same procedures. These differ considerably from the GCCF rules and shows are run in a totally different way. In Britain, the CA is very much the minority group, as the GCCF runs approximately 90% of all shows. The GCCF is the oldest governing body in the world, as the cat fancy started in Britain. For this reason it retained its own rules and regulations rather than becoming affiliated to the FIFe.

It is impossible to show pedigree cats at both GCCF and CA shows, as the GCCF rules clearly state that no GCCF-registered cat may be shown at a non-GCCF show unless special permission has been granted. As non-pedigree cats are not registered at all, however, it is quite possible to show them under both organisations. You should still take care not to break the GCCF's 13-day rule, as this applies whatever show your cat has attended. It should also be mentioned that at present there are movements afoot among GCCF exhibitors to start a register of non-pedigree cats, so things may change in the future. It is possible to register your non-pedigree cat with the CA.

The FIFe has a standard for household pet cats similar to the standards for pedigree cats. In the case of household pets (HPs) the standard mainly concerns health and temperament. The rules for showing your HP within the CA are:

- It must have been vaccinated not more than 12 months or less than 14 days before the show.
- Its claws must have been trimmed prior to the show.
- If adult, it must be neutered.

Within the FIFe, cats are classified as adult at the age of ten months, as opposed to nine within the GCCF, and eight in most American clubs.

Your cat has to go through a vetting-in procedure upon arrival at the show similar to that at the GCCF shows. The CA is very particular that its veterinary rules are observed at all times and a copy of these can be obtained from the CA. The FIFe has no rule concerning how often a cat can be shown, and many of its shows (especially in other countries) are two-day events.

At CA shows, the cat pens are all 120cm x 60cm (4ft x 2ft), and these can be decorated however the owner wishes, as no judging takes place at the pens. Normally they are furnished with special drapes covering the back and sides of the pen, some sort of floor covering, possibly a bed, and a litter tray, water bowl and food bowl. You need to bring your own cat litter and food for your cat.

You will be given a tally for your cat to wear around its neck, tied either with ribbon or elastic. Chairs are provided at all CA shows so that you can sit down in front of your cat's pen. You can also sit in front of the judging area to watch the judging.

At CA shows there are trophies and special rosettes for the Best Longhaired Pet, the Best Shorthaired Pet and the Best Overall Pet. There are also special awards: the Laureate Awards. To qualify for these, your cat must be registered with the CA, and you must be a member. The first level is the CA Laureate, and to achieve this award your pet has to gain a CAL certificate on three separate occasions under three different judges. The CAL certificate is a card with a Union Flag on it, bearing the cat's name and the date and venue of the show at which the certificate was awarded. Once your cat has won three, you can apply to the CA's Show Division for the title of CA Laureate for your cat. This title is added in front of your cat's name, usually in the form of the letters CAL, just as a champion pedigree cat has the letters Ch in front of its name.

The second level of special awards is the CA Laureate Prima, for which your cat must be awarded a CALP certificate five times under three different judges. The third level is the CA Laureate Suprema. To achieve this title, your cat must win its class and be awarded the CALS certificate seven times under at least three different judges. Finally, the highest honour a household pet cat can gain is the title CA Laureate Imperata (CALI). To achieve this, your cat needs to win ten CALS certificates under at least three different judges.

Once you have claimed each title for your cat you will be able to order special rosettes with the title printed on them.

THE INDEPENDENT FELINE ALLIANCE (IFA)

The Independent Feline Alliance (IFA) was founded in 1994 as an alternative showing system with equal opportunities for all cats and kittens. All cats can compete for titles, even kittens and non-pedigrees. Whether your cat is a household pet or a pedigree, it does not have to be registered to be exhibited at an IFA show.

The IFA has no controlling or supervisory body or committee; it is a co-operative of independent cat clubs that have come together to promote the health and welfare of all felines and to provide all cat lovers wishing to show their cats with a simple and enjoyable championship system. Each club retains its own independence and there are no rules with which a club must comply - just an agreement that any show staged under the IFA banner is conducted in accordance with the commonly agreed 'Code of Practice'.

The IFA uses a 'Three-ring Open System' at its shows. A ring is simply an area where a judge is seated by a table, and all the cats are brought to the table. The Three-ring Open System means that there are three different judges for each open class so, technically, a cat can become a fully-made-up champion during just one show if it wins its open class under all three judges. Exhibitors can watch their cats being judged, listen to what the judge has to say, and receive a written critique. All exhibits compete for Challenge Certificates.

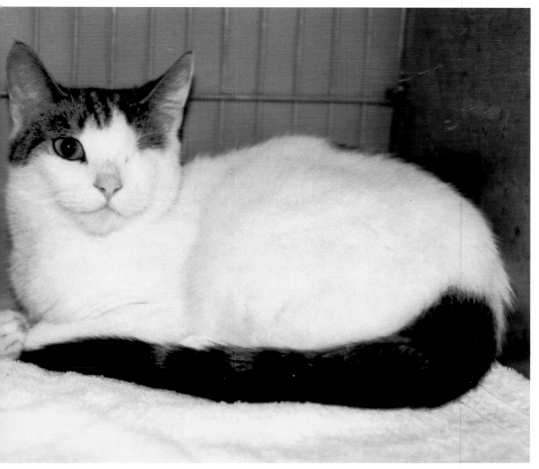

Some cat clubs have classes for disabled cats such as one-eyed Nelson at their shows.

Kittens have to be at least three calendar months old, and all cats entered must have been vaccinated no less than 15 days prior to the show. (Technically, this would be difficult to meet in the case of a kitten which usually receives its second injection at the age of 12 weeks, so would be at least 14 weeks old before it could be shown.)

All non-pedigree cats older than 10 months must be neutered. No cat that has been present at any other cat show during the last 12 days can be entered. Needless to say, all cats arriving at the show are carefully examined by a qualified veterinary surgeon before being allowed into the hall.

There are several different categories for household pets:

- Part Pedigrees have one pedigree and one moggy parent.
- Cross pedigrees have parents of two different pedigree breeds.
- Pedigree pets are pure-bred cats of pet quality; in other words, they have one or more faults that prevent them from competing as pedigrees.
- Domestic pets are moggies.

The age limits are:
- Kitten   3-9 months
- Junior   10-14 months
- Adult   15 months and over
- Veteran   6-9 years
- Vintage   10 years and over

Apart from the open classes, all cats can compete in various side classes, such as 'Largest paws' and 'Most feminine female'. There are also special classes for disabled or handicapped cats. The cats are housed in 120cm x 60cm (4ft x 2ft) pens, which can be decorated, and there are prizes for the best decorated ones. A litter tray and a bowl of water must always be provided for the cat. Two cats or up to four kittens from the same household may share a pen. Prizes are guaranteed for each cat: one rosette for each class entered.

THE INDEPENDENT PET CAT SOCIETY (TIPCS)

The Independent Pet Cat Society (TIPCS), a breakaway group from the CA, was formed in 1985. Its shows are open to all cats, including pedigrees and part-pedigrees, but all cats are judged as household pets. In other words, the criteria are condition, grooming and temperament. There are many champion titles to compete for, from Champion all the way up to Imperial Grand Champion. As within the IFA, each cat is judged in three different rings for its open class. All open class judges give a written critique of each cat. For the purpose of the open classes, the cats are separated into Longhair and shorthair groups, which are then divided into pure-bred, half-pedigree and domestic pet classes. Large classes may be divided further by age or sex. There are also side classes which are judged at the cats' pens rather than in a ring. These may include classes such as reduced cat or kitten, area classes, club and charity classes.

Within the TIPCS, adult cats are defined as 15 months and over, and only these can compete for championship awards. The winner of each adult open class is given a Champion Pet Merit Award. Three of these earn the cat the title of Champion Pet.

Cats between the ages of 9 and 15 months may compete for Junior Champion Pet titles, and they also need a minimum of three awards.

The pens for the cats are each 60cm x 60cm (2ft x 2ft) and can be decorated as the owners wish. Seats are provided so that the exhibitors can watch the judging.

Every cat entered for a TIPCS show has to be vetted in upon arrival and vaccination must not have taken place later than seven days before the show. Kittens must be at least three months old on the show day. No cat that has attended any other cat show less than 13 days prior to the show can be entered, and nor can any other cat from the household affected.

Children delight in their pets winning prizes.

In the open classes, cats and kittens are judged on a points system. The overall top score is 50 points, which is divided into 25 points for condition, 15 for temperament and 10 for presentation (grooming). The cat with the highest number of points is the winner. If more than one cat has the same number of points the judge has to choose the winner. To ensure that the high standard is maintained, champion cats cannot receive a merit award unless they have received a minimum number of merit points: 40 for Junior Champion or Champion and 43 for Grand Champion.

THE LAUREATE CAT CLUB (LCC)

The Laureate Cat Club is another club purely for pet cats. The LCC defines a pet cat as any non-pedigree cat, any cat not registered with any national or international body representing cats (except the LCC), or any cat registered with a national or international body but purchased and kept by its owner solely as a pet - not used for breeding or shown in the pedigree section of any show.

The LCC is independent of all other organisations and runs cat shows throughout the year. The club also sponsors classes at certain nominated shows during the year, making awards which enable pet cats to gain titles such as Champion. The LCC also intends that pet cats can achieve these awards through other organisations, so that your pet cat could become a champion within the LCC by winning at shows run by other organisations. The club also sponsors the welfare of all cats and the neutering of cats not being used as part of a viable breeding programme.

There are many stages of awards, starting from Ribbon when a cat has been awarded a first, second or third in an open class on three separate occasions at any show anywhere in the UK, up to Roll of Honour when the cat has to achieve a certain number of wins during a two-year period. The higher stages have to include wins at LCC or LCC-nominated shows.

At LCC shows, the ring judging system is used throughout. Cats in the open classes are judged according to a points system where the overall total is 100 points. The points are divided as follows:

• Condition	50 points (subdivided into parts such as body and tail, head and ears)
• Personality and temperament	30 points
• Presentation	20 points

The open class winner is the cat or kitten with the highest number of points. In the case of two cats with the same number of points the judge must choose one winner. Each cat in the open classes receives a written critique. There are also miscellaneous classes, such as Rescued. There are special 'Cats of courage' classes for handicapped and disabled cats. Wherever possible, cats with similar disabilities compete against each other but otherwise are judged in the same way as all other cats.

SHOWING PET CATS IN THE UNITED STATES OF AMERICA

Showing household pet cats (known as HHPs) in the United States is quite different from in Britain. There are five main governing bodies and rules vary from club to club. In general, it can be said that any cat can be shown as an HHP, whether it is an ordinary moggy or a pedigree cat that does not meet the criteria for its own breed.

In the USA, many shows are two-day events, known as back-to-back shows, where you may be able to show your cat twice within the two days.

Cats are generally shown in pens 60cm x 60cm (2ft x 2ft). These can be decorated however the owner wishes, but the back and sides should always be covered. If you do not have special show drapes you can use large bath towels.

The American Cat Fanciers Association Inc

The ACFA is very interested in pet cats and has an HHP class at each show, where any cat, background known or unknown, can be exhibited. The Association registers pedigree cats and records household pets. A pure-bred cat may be recorded as an HHP provided that its pedigree registration is surrendered at the time of recording. If a pedigree cat is to be recorded as an HHP and the owner wishes to continue to use the cat's 'official' name, including the breeder's cattery name (prefix), the breeder will have to sign the form, stating that he or she has no objection to this name being used. After this, the cat may never again be shown in pedigree classes.

When you record your HHP with the Association you have to fill in a form stating whether your cat is of mixed breeding or pure breeding, together with such details as colour and age, and you have to confirm that your cat has been neutered, stating when and at which surgery or centre.

HHP kittens are classified as between four and eight months of age. Any HHP that has reached eight months must be neutered ('altered' in American English).

HHPs do not have to be recorded with the ACFA to be eligible for exhibition, but only those that are can compete for the various titles on offer for pet cats. These are known as 'Titles of Merit' and are similar to those awarded to pedigree cats. Titles are earned under a system in which points are awarded according to the cat's final placings at shows. Cats are judged in rings and, although they are only entered in one class (no side classes), can be judged by more than one judge on the same day. HHP titles are listed below and range from Royal (the lowest of the Royal Household Pet group) to Supreme Roll of Honour (highest of the Supreme Household Pet group).

Champagne Charlie, stable-mate of Kit Carson, also started life as a rescued cat and became a show winner.

In the Royal Household Pet group the titles are:	In the Supreme Household Pet group they are:
• Royal • Double Royal • Triple Royal	• Supreme • Double Supreme • Triple Supreme • Quadruple Supreme • Supreme Roll of Honour

You need to keep a record of your cat's wins and, once the correct number of points has been won, you can apply for the appropriate title from the ACFA office. In some cases, a small fee is asked for confirmation of a title. For the higher titles special certificates are available for a fee. The full list of titles and points is printed in each show catalogue. The ACFA also offer special end-of-year awards for household pets.

The Cat Fanciers' Federation Inc

A household pet within the CFF is usually of mixed breeding but can be a pedigree cat that has failed to meet the show criteria for its breed, for example, having a kinked tail, crossed eyes or a colour fault.

Any household pet over the age of eight months must be neutered. The minimum age for exhibition is four months. Household pets must meet the same basic show standards as any of the pedigree cats in the show. They must be healthy, have up-to-date vaccination certificates (including against rabies) and be free of parasites. The cat must be bathed and groomed thoroughly before the show, including having its front and back claws trimmed and its eyes, ears and teeth cleaned. This club has the welcome rule that neither de-clawed nor de-vocalised cats can be shown.

Cats at CFF shows are judged according to health, temperament, beauty and personality. Any cat that meets the show requirements receives a 'Merit' ribbon and from the merit winners the judge picks 10 cats for the finals. Some clubs divide the household pet entries into different classes but this largely depends upon the number of entries received.

Household pets can be registered officially with the CFF and are then eligible to compete for HHP titles. The title Companion is awarded to an HHP that has reached the finals in any ring. The range then goes through Grand Companion (a cat that is a confirmed Companion and has reached the finals in five rings under at least three different judges) up to Master Grand Companion (a cat that has been in six finals and won one Best Cat under three different judges). A confirmation fee will be payable for each title, and most of these include a rosette and a certificate. Household Pets can also compete for annual awards, and there are listings of the 'Top 20 Household Pets' during each show year.

The American Cat Association Inc

The ACA, the first of all American registries, was founded in 1897 by Lady Marcus Beresford of England. The ACA was the first association in America to register household pets. In 1993 titles for household pets were introduced: Companion Cat, Grand Companion Cat and Master Grand Companion Cat. Within the ACA, household pets and pedigree cats are always judged by the same judges and receive the same value prizes and the same quality rosettes. All household pets compete on equal terms, whether they are kittens or adults, mixed breeds or 'pure-breed look-alike'. All household pets over the age of eight months must be neutered. A cat can only be shown as a household pet if it is of mixed breeding or a pedigree that never has been registered as such.

Others
There are two more major bodies in the USA, The Independent Cat Association (TICA) and the Cat Fanciers' Association (CFA). Sadly, at the time of writing I do not know whether they organise shows that include non-pedigree cats.

CONTACTING THE CAT CLUBS
Clubs' officers (and therefore their contact addresses) often change so it is impractical to list them all in this book. Anybody wishing to contact any of the clubs mentioned can write to me, Marianne Mays, c/o TFH/Kingdom Books, and I will endeavour to send you an up-to-date address for the club you wish to contact. Please enclose a stamped, addressed envelope or an international reply coupon.

Felicia wins yet another show, with a steward standing in for owner Rebecca Mays.

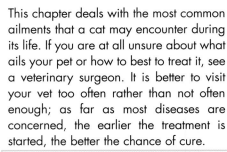

chapter
seven
health care

This chapter deals with the most common ailments that a cat may encounter during its life. If you are at all unsure about what ails your pet or how to best to treat it, see a veterinary surgeon. It is better to visit your vet too often rather than not often enough; as far as most diseases are concerned, the earlier the treatment is started, the better the chance of cure.

Always remember that a happy, healthy cat should be:

- neutered
- vaccinated annually
- wormed several times a year
- checked regularly for fleas, ear mites and other external parasites

Any cat denied any of these runs a risk of being taken seriously ill sooner or later.

EATING PROBLEMS
Diarrhoea
Symptoms: The motions (faeces) are much softer than usual, perhaps even liquid and in severe cases you may find drops of liquid diarrhoea outside the litter tray. The smell is much worse than usual. The cat often appears perfectly normal in every other respect and still want to eat. In very severe cases, or if the cat is suffering from another disease, it may appear listless and generally unwell.

Cause: Many cats are sensitive to cow's milk, and this should be cut out of the diet immediately. Specially formulated milk drinks are available but no adult cat needs to drink milk - water is far better. Diarrhoea can also be caused by stress, bowel infections, diseases such as Feline Leukaemia Virus, a change in the diet, worms, and even excessive eating.

Treatment: First leave the cat without food for 12 to 24 hours to let its stomach settle down; any food increases the problem. The cat must have access to water at all times. If by then the cat has not passed any motions, give it small amounts of chicken, turkey or boiled fish - no more than half the usual amount. Cottage cheese is also suitable. Gradually increase the amount and slowly re-introduce small portions of the cat's normal food with the diet food. If the diarrhoea persists or the cat appears at all unwell see a vet. The cat must not go untreated for long, as it could become dehydrated, with severe consequences. If the cat vomits as well as having diarrhoea, see a vet at once.

Constipation

Symptoms: The cat strains but produces little or no faeces, sometimes passing spots of blood. The motions, if any, are very hard. Occasionally, small amounts of liquid faeces are passed, which can be mistaken for diarrhoea. A constipated cat often refuses to eat, may be generally unwell, and is usually very upset if its anus is touched, as this will hurt. If the constipation is really bad or has been allowed to go on for some time, the cat's stomach may appear swollen, and it may start to vomit because the cat is beginning to absorb toxins from the hard motions retained in the bowel for too long.

Cause: The cat may have swallowed a furball which has caused a blockage. Outdoor cats may have swallowed bones or bird feathers which could also cause constipation.

Treatment: Give the cat 2-5ml (a half to one teaspoonful) of medicinal paraffin oil either by syringe or by spoon. If this has no effect, see a vet. Surgery will be necessary if something like a bone is lodged in the cat's stomach. If your cat often suffers from constipation add extra roughage to its food, such as a teaspoonful of bran.

Gingivitis

Symptoms: The cat's gums are red and inflamed and may bleed easily, and the cat has bad breath. In severe cases the cat may drool and find it painful to eat.

Cause: This condition can be caused by a build-up of tartar on the cat's teeth causing inflamed and sore gums, irritant substances being licked from the cat's coat, an infection or even too much Vitamin A.

Treatment: See a vet, who will prescribe either antibiotics or something to be applied to the cat's gums. Tartar and any very bad teeth may be removed under anaesthetic.

Vomiting

Cause: Cats sometimes vomit for no apparent reason or to expel furballs. As long as it is not frequent and the cat appears well there is no need for concern. However, if a cat vomits frequently (four times during a 24-hour period), it may have picked up an infection, been poisoned, or swallowed a foreign body. It could also simply be greedy and have eaten too much! Vomiting may also occur as a result of travel sickness and as a symptom of many diseases and conditions, including severe constipation.

Treatment: Cats sometimes need to vomit to clean out their stomach and to do this, they eat grass or similar substances. An indoor cat may start to eat houseplants but you must watch out for this, as many houseplants are toxic for cats. If your cat is vomiting frequently for no apparent reason and is generally lethargic, see a vet as soon as possible. If the cat is vomiting because it is eating too much, give it smaller portions several times a day rather than two large meals. Remember that food should be served at room temperature rather than straight from the fridge.

Dehydration

Symptoms: It is important to know how to detect this. Pinch the skin at the back of the cat's neck, and lift it up. When you release it, it should fall back into place immediately. If it only moves slowly, or stays in the same position, the cat is dehydrated.

Cause: There can be various causes, but it is often a result of acute vomiting and diarrhoea.

Treatment: Consult a vet as soon as possible.

WOUNDS AND ABSCESSES

Cause: Wounds are probably received during a fight with another cat. Small puncture wounds can be difficult to spot, and have a tendency to turn into abscesses. An abscess can be seen as a swelling anywhere on the cat's body, and is painful to the touch. As it matures it increases in size and may burst, emitting a foul-smelling mixture of pus and blood. At this stage, it is less painful to the cat.

Treatment: Always treat any wound that you find using a mild antiseptic or soap and warm water to prevent abscesses from forming. If an abscess has formed, a vet will have to lance and flush out the abscess and the cat will need antibiotics.

EAR PROBLEMS

Ear infection (*Otitis externa*)

Symptoms: The cat scratches its ears, and may hold them flat down to the head. The scratching may make the fur around the ear thin out, and the skin outside and inside the ear sore and even bleed. The ear smells bad and there is sometimes a discharge.

Cause: Ear infections can arise from fight wounds, foreign bodies inside the ear or ear mites. They may also develop as a direct result of the owner having tried to clean the ear canal, which should never be touched unless there is a problem.

Treatment: Carefully clean the ear with cotton buds dampened with water or a little baby oil. If you can see a foreign body, remove it if possible. If the ear appears very dirty and inflamed, see a vet, who will prescribe ear drops.

Ear mites

Symptoms: A very dark, almost black, dry, crusty discharge is seen inside the cat's ear. The cat will scratch, maybe causing the ear to bleed. Even if the ear has just been cleaned out, a quick shake of the cat's head may cause more mites to appear, as they live at the bottom of the ear, where no cotton bud can reach.

Cause: A small mite by the name of *Otodectes synotis* that lives in the ear canal. Ear mites are often seen in outdoor cats as they spread easily from cat to cat.

Treatment: Ear drops from the vet. It is important to clean the cat's ears daily, as the drops do not do much good on their own. Use cotton buds dipped in baby oil, which suffocates the mites and also helps to get out all the dry matter.

Ear haematoma

Symptoms: The cat's ear flap is swollen, either completely or in part.

Cause: Blood blister: a small vessel in the ear flap has burst, causing a blood-filled swelling. Often the result of a fight with another cat, but can also be caused by the cat shaking its head or scratching its ear vigorously because of an infection.

Treatment: If the haematoma is fairly small, rub an ice-cube against it for a few minutes twice a day. If the swelling does not reduce, a vet may have to drain the ear under general anaesthetic, stitching the ear tightly to prevent the haematoma from reappearing. An untreated haematoma will eventually cause the ear to contract and become distorted in shape, something often referred to as 'cauliflower ear' or 'boxer's ear'.

EYE PROBLEMS

Conjunctivitis

Symptoms: The eye discharges copiously and appears red (especially around the rims) and swollen. The discharge is either clear or in the form of yellow or green pus.

Cause: This condition can be caused by a foreign body in the eye, an injury, an infection, an infectious disease, an allergy, an accidental poke in the eye, or simply by the cat sitting in a bad draught.

Treatment: See your vet, who will establish the cause of the infection and prescribe appropriate drops or ointment.

PARASITES (INTERNAL)

Worms

Symptoms: The worms can often be seen in the cat's faeces, in vomit or around the tail and anus.

> * Roundworms are 3-10cm long, round and slender, with tapered ends.
> * Tapeworms can be longer, but are usually seen as small segments, each 0.5-1cm long. The segments are flat and, when dry, look like grains of rice. Tapeworms are often detected when dried ones are found in the cat's bed.

A cat with worms often has a 'pot belly' (distended stomach but thin back, with the backbone clearly visible) and a dull coat. It will probably have a poor appetite, as its stomach is full of worms, not leaving enough room for food.

Cause: Worms are common in outdoor cats, especially if they hunt and eat wildlife, but they can affect indoor cats. Tapeworms can occur as a result of flea infestation; the cat swallows fleas and flea eggs carrying tapeworm eggs and is thus infected.

Treatment: All cats should be wormed regularly, two to four times a year, depending on whether they are allowed out. Tablets from your vet are far more effective than any that can be bought over the counter. Your vet can supply you with tablets that will kill off both roundworms and tapeworms in one single dose. Take great care to give the correct dose, which should be according to your cat's weight. Follow your vet's instructions.

Toxoplasmosis

Symptoms: Most cats show no symptoms at all. If there are any they may include high temperatures, rapid breathing and diarrhoea. It can be fatal to kittens. In adult cats there may also be weight loss, wobbliness, pale membranes and possibly blindness.

Cause: A single-cell parasite by the name of *Toxoplasma gondii*. This disease is fairly common in cats, and can be transferred to humans. The health risk is small, and a person with the disease may believe it to be a mild form of flu. However, there is a threat to the unborn child so pregnant women should avoid handling cat litter trays; the disease is spread mainly through infected cats' faeces, although it can also be spread by unwashed vegetables and raw meat. An infected person can be treated successfully with antibiotics. The cat itself has usually caught the infection from other animals that it has killed and eaten, so outdoor cats are at much greater risk than indoor ones.

Treatment: See a vet, who will be able to confirm the disease by blood tests and examination of cat's faeces. The disease can then be treated with antibiotics.

PARASITES (EXTERNAL) AND OTHER SKIN PROBLEMS

Fleas

Symptoms: Fleas can be seen moving around the body of a badly-infested cat, especially around the face and along the back. Each flea is dark brown in colour, and measures from 2-4mm. Flea dirt can be seen very clearly on a pale-coloured cat, but perhaps not quite so easily on a dark one. Flea dirt comes in small, dry, dark specks which appear black but, being dried blood, turn red when moistened.

Cause: Most cats are infested with fleas at some point in their lives, especially those that have outdoor access. Longhaired cats often suffer worse than shorthaired ones, as fleas seem to prefer long fur. Fleas are especially prevalent during warm weather and everything possible should be done to keep them under control.

Treatment: Fleas cause great discomfort (some cats are allergic to flea bites), could lead to tapeworms, and sometimes bite people, even if they do not live on them. There are many good flea sprays available from vets and chemists. Flea powder can be used, but usually this is not quite as effective as spray. Flea collars are available, but give some cats skin irritations. There are even tablets to give to cats which control fleas by rendering them infertile. Ask your vet for advice. A flea comb is useful, as it picks up fleas and flea dirt. Always follow the manufacturer's instructions when using any anti-flea treatment. Many cannot be used on young kittens and should be avoided on pregnant cats.

It is also important to treat the cat's environment, as fleas live in carpets and bedding. Regular vacuuming is recommended. There are special sprays available for carpets and bedding (**never** to be used on the cat itself) and also various 'flea-traps' that work with lights and sticky discs to attract and trap the fleas.

Ringworm

Symptoms: They vary, but the cat may have small scratch-like lesions with yellowish dandruff, especially around its ears, neck and face. The classical ringworm symptoms are circular lesions, 0.5-2.5cm in diameter, in which the centre of the lesion is clear skin, giving the impression of a circle. Humans can catch it and the lesions are very obvious on bare skin. It causes bad itching on humans and a certain amount on cats.

Cause: This is not a worm as the name suggests, but a fungus. It spreads through contact with contaminated animals, but also indirectly through spores carried on clothes and bedding. The spores are very tough and may live for as long as a couple of years in the right environment.

Treatment: A vet checks for ringworm spores on the cat by means of a Wood's lamp (a light with ultra-violet rays which change to fluorescent green if ringworm spores are present) and cultures grown from fur samples taken from the cat. The Wood's lamp is not 100% reliable so, if it gives a positive result, a culture must be grown as well. If no spores have grown within 10 days the cat can be considered clear.

A picture of health – but beware of fleas and other infestations.

The cat is bathed or sprayed twice a week and put on medication. The tablets usually given to cats with ringworm must **never** be given to pregnant queens. Give the tablets with some sort of fat so that they are more readily absorbed. Some people advocate shaving affected cats, but the actual shaving process can irritate the cat's skin. Regular bathing is a much better option. All cats in the same household have to be treated, whether they show any symptoms or not, as spores may be carried on their fur. It is also important to clean the cat's environment. Your vet will advise you on this. The cat is normally kept on medication for four to six weeks. Once all lesions are gone, the cat is tested once again for ringworm spores before it is finally cleared.

Feline acne

Symptoms/Cause: The skin is irritated in places, usually on the chin. Excess dirt and oil block the pores, causing pimples and small abscesses, similar to acne in humans.

Treatment: Your vet will prescribe ointment and possibly antibiotics.

Skin cancer

Symptoms: The edges of the cat's ears become red and sore and the fur starts to fall out. Eventually, the ears become hairless, permanently red and prone to bleeding. The whole process may take years and the cat is usually better during winter and autumn. Eventually the ears may curl, the skin flake off and the ears itch and bleed very easily.

Cause: Cats with white or very pale ears are prone to sunburn in the summer, because of the lack of pigmentation in the skin, and this can lead to skin cancer of the ears.

Treatment: See a vet. In bad cases, the ears will have to be amputated to prevent the cancer from spreading. Prevention is always best, so keep a pale-eared cat out of the direct sun as much as possible and apply a sun-blocking cream during summer.

URINARY PROBLEMS
Feline Urological Syndrome (FUS)

This fairly common condition in both male and female cats should always be regarded as serious, as the condition may occasionally be fatal, especially in male cats. FUS involves an inflammation of the bladder and urethra, and the formation of sand or grit-like crystals in the cat's urine. In male cats the urethra is long and narrow, with a bend in it which can become blocked. In females, the urethra is shorter and broader, which means that it very rarely becomes blocked.

Symptoms: The cat squats frequently, strains, but does not manage to urinate. It will probably lick its penis or vulva. The cat may produce small amounts of urine frequently, sometimes in places where it would not normally urinate. Sometimes blood may be seen in the urine. If the urethra is partially or completely blocked, a male cat may be lethargic, with a swollen abdomen, and may cry in pain when handled. Sometimes the penis may be protruding, showing a red, swollen tip.

Cause: There can be several causes, or a combination of factors: infections, too much magnesium in the diet, the cat not drinking enough water, too much dry food and reduced physical activity. If the cat has restricted or no access to the place where it normally urinates, it may hold its urine, causing stale urine to remain in the bladder.

Treatment: See a vet as soon as possible. If treatment is delayed, the cat may die, because of a toxic waste build-up in the blood or a ruptured bladder. The vet will put the cat under general anaesthetic and clear the blockage. Afterwards, the cat will receive medication and be put on a special diet recommended by your vet. Should the problem recur, surgery can be performed to shorten the urethra in males.

Cystitis

Symptoms: The cat urinates more frequently than normal, but only produces a few drops of urine. The urine may be blood-stained and the cat may squat in places where it does not normally urinate. It will lick its genital area. The cat spends a much longer time than usual trying to pass urine, although smaller amounts are produced.

Cause: This is caused by inflammation of the bladder and can be confused and/or associated with FUS in male cats. In female cats, the cause is usually a contamination of the vulva by bacteria, but can also be due to FUS. If the cat doesn't urinate for a long time, for whatever reason, stale urine retained in the bladder provides an ideal breeding ground for bacteria. Bacteria can be picked up from dirty litter trays when cats urinate so keep the trays as clean as possible.

Treatment: See a vet as soon as possible. Antibiotic treatment will be needed. It is important to get the cat to drink as much as possible, as this will flush out bacteria from the bladder. In severe cases, the vet may have to X-ray the cat to find whether bladder stones, or even a tumour, are present.

KIDNEY DISEASE

If the kidneys fail to function properly, waste products accumulate in the cat's bloodstream, producing a toxic effect that could prove fatal. There are two main types of kidney disease: chronic and acute.

Acute kidney disease

Symptoms: This is most common in cats aged six years or under. Acute kidney disease is distinguished from chronic kidney disease by the sudden onset of very obvious symptoms. The cat refuses to eat, although it may still show some interest in food. Normally it drinks much more than usual, although in certain cases it may actually drink less. Vomiting may occur, leading to dehydration. The cat is lethargic and appears dull and unkempt as it will stop grooming itself.

Cause: The causes can vary: infection, kidney damage resulting from an accident, poisoning, or as a result of another disease or condition.

Treatment: See a vet who will do a blood test to diagnose the disease. If the cat is becoming dehydrated it may have to be kept at the surgery for treatment. As the cat recovers it must be fed on a low protein diet that will not put undue strain on the kidneys. Such diets are available from vets in the form of canned or dry food.

Chronic kidney disease

Symptoms: Chronic kidney disease often develops so slowly that it can be months or even years before the cat appears to be ill. It drinks more than usual and urinates more frequently. The urine may have a stronger smell. The cat often loses weight gradually and may be lethargic. It vomits occasionally and probably has bad breath. It may also cease to groom itself as well as it normally does. It can be difficult to tell whether anything is wrong, as the cat may seem perfectly healthy for long periods of time.

Cause: Very common in older cats. The cause is often unidentified, but it can arise as a result of another disease or condition.

Treatment: See a vet, who will diagnose the disease by a blood test and possibly also urine samples. The cat's diet will need to be changed to a low protein one available from the vet, and medication may be prescribed, depending on how ill the cat is. If kept on this type of diet, most cats with chronic kidney disease can live quite happily for several more years.

FELINE INFLUENZA OR CAT FLU

Two types of virus are commonly known as Cat Flu: Feline Viral Rhinotracheitis (FVR) and Feline Calicivirus (FCV). Sometimes they are both seen at once in the same cat. Prevent the disease from occurring by having your cat vaccinated every year.

Feline Viral Rhinotracheitis (FVR)

Symptoms: The cat seems lethargic and has a high temperature (normal temperature for a cat is around 38.5°C). Other symptoms are sneezing and discharges from the nose and eyes. The eyes may become inflamed. The cat will probably refuse to eat, and it may drool and cough. Eventually it could lose weight and become dehydrated.

Cause: Highly contagious herpes virus, which can be spread either by direct or indirect contact.

Treatment: See a vet as soon as possible for antibiotics. If not treated in time, the cat will die. A cat that recovers may retain some chronic problems such as snuffling and sneezing. A sick cat must be isolated from other cats and needs extra tempting to eat and drink.

Feline Calicivirus (FCV)

Symptoms: The cat is lethargic, has a high temperature and refuses its food. There is a clear discharge from the eyes and nose, and the cat will probably dribble because of ulcers forming on its tongue. The disease can be fatal.

Cause: A virus spread by either direct or indirect contact.

Treatment: See a vet as soon as possible. Treatment is very much the same as for Feline Viral Rhinotracheitis.

OTHER INFECTIOUS DISEASES
Feline Infectious Enteritis (FIE) or Feline Panleucopaenia

Symptoms: Diarrhoea and vomiting, lethargy and fluctuating temperature. The diarrhoea and vomiting will soon make the cat dehydrated. The cat will probably have some abdominal pain and may sit hunched up because of this.

Cause: Very contagious virus. The disease is fatal in most cases, and prevention should be by vaccination. As many as 90% of young cats affected by this disease die without even showing any symptoms, some within 24 hours of contracting the virus. The virus is spread either directly or indirectly, so even cats kept indoors are at risk.

Treatment: See a vet as soon as possible, but the outcome is usually fatal.

Feline Leukaemia Virus (FeLV)

Symptoms: The most normal is cancer of the lymph system, but it may also involve other organs. Symptoms may include poor appetite, weight loss, vomiting, diarrhoea, breathing problems, lethargy and weakness. Queens may give birth to dead or sickly kittens or abort the litter. Some cats die after exposure to the virus, others recover after a period of time, and a small number become symptomless carriers.

Cause: A virus passed on from affected cats. This can be through bites, mating, mutual washing, or sharing litter trays and food bowls. FeLV is quite common, and any cat allowed outdoors will be at risk, unless vaccinated.

Treatment: The disease is untreatable so prevention is better than cure. Any cat allowed outdoors must be vaccinated. Pedigree cats used for breeding are always blood-tested before being allowed to mate. Any cat about to be vaccinated against FeLV should be blood-tested first, to ensure that it is free from the disease. Any new cat introduced to the household should also be blood-tested to ensure that it is not a carrier.

Feline Infectious Peritonitis (FIP)

Symptoms: Poor appetite, with weight loss and lethargy. The cat's abdomen may be swollen or it may develop breathing problems, depending which part of the body is affected.

Cause: This is a virus, more commonly seen in young cats.

Treatment: Cats with FIP usually die within six weeks. A cat suspected of having FIP can be blood-tested for the presence of corona virus anti-bodies in its blood, but the only sure confirmation is by autopsy after the cat's death. No vaccine is available.

Feline Immunodeficiency Virus (FIV)

Symptoms: The most usual symptoms are poor appetite, weight loss, fluctuating temperature, swollen glands, mouth infections, breathing problems and diarrhoea. As the immune system fails, other diseases may result.

Cause: This is the feline version of the human HIV. The virus is species specific, only affecting cats. It is spread mainly through biting. The cats at greatest risk are unneutered toms that regularly get into fights. No vaccine is available.

Treatment: A vet will confirm the disease by blood test. All new cats introduced into a household should be blood-tested for the presence of FIV. No treatment is available, and infected cats may live for years, posing a serious threat to healthy cats. A FIV-infected cat can be kept until it falls ill and starts to suffer, but this must be in a household with no other cat and no outdoor access.

chapter

eight

cat behaviour

There will always come a point in a cat owner's life when he or she wonders, 'Now, **why** does my cat behave like this?' Cats are fairly complicated animals with a large range of behavioural patterns and a whole secret language of their own. In many respects, the domesticated cat, especially the non-pedigree, is still a wild animal sharing our homes. Most of its behavioural patterns can be traced back to when it really was wild. This chapter is intended as a rough guide to some of the behavioural patterns that may be seen in the domestic cat. It is not intended as an in-depth study. For anyone interested in finding out more about cat behaviour, many specialist books on this subject are available and I would strongly recommend that you read one.

PURRING

Most people will immediately associate a purring cat with a happy and contented mood. To a large extent, this is true: a happy cat will purr, and there is nothing quite as pleasant as having a cat or kitten purring away on your lap. However, a cat in great distress, such as intense pain, or even a female cat giving birth, will also purr. It is an interesting fact that only friendly cats in pain purr when approached by people, which seems to suggest that cats purr to show that they are friendly and approachable, ready to be stroked or helped.

Kittens start to purr as early as two to three days after the birth, although it has often been suggested that this will not happen until they are two to three weeks old. Anyone who has bred and reared

kittens will know that they purr as early as two days after they have been born - only you need good hearing to realise this! As the kittens grow older, the purr grows louder. The purring shows that the kittens are contented and getting enough food when suckling, providing a signal to the mother cat that all is well.

Exactly how cats purr has still not been established; it is as yet something of a mystery, though various theories have been put forward.

JUMPING UP ON ITS HIND LEGS TO GREET ITS OWNER

Many cats jump up on their hind legs when greeting their owners or friends; indeed, I have one that greets our dogs like that. This is simply a case of the cat trying to reach the person's face. Cats normally greet each other by rubbing faces and this is what the cat is trying to achieve. If the person in question lowers his or her face to the cat's level, the cat will rub faces with the person.

ROLLING ONTO ITS BACK WHEN IT SEES ITS OWNER

The cat rolls onto its back, stretching its legs out as far as possible, yawning and exercising its claws. This is another friendly way for a cat to greet its owner, and it usually only happens with its immediate family (never with strangers). This sort of greeting indicates total trust of the person in question; the 'belly up' posture is a very vulnerable one. It is also a fairly lazy way of greeting its owner; a more active cat will probably run up and rub against its owner's legs.

RUBBING AGAINST OWNER'S LEGS

Yet another form of greeting, where the cat is rubbing off some of its scent on its owner. Cats have scent glands on the temples, around the mouth and at the base of the tail, although it is a smell that only other cats can sense.

KNEADING

This is when the cat extends and retracts its claws, usually when resting on its owner's lap. The behaviour stems from kittenhood; kittens knead whilst suckling their mothers to make the milk flow more easily. Many adult cats will do this when they feel contented. They see their owners as surrogate mothers and, as pampered pets, they often retain certain kitten characteristics even in adult life. If this behaviour is seen with dribbling and perhaps sucking of the owner's clothes or hair, the cat was probably weaned too young and never had a chance to grow out of this behaviour naturally. Such a cat retains this behavioural pattern for life. It is often seen in non-pedigree cats, as so many are taken from their mothers at far too early an age.

PHLEMING

This is when the cat screws up its face, baring its upper teeth slightly by raising the upper lips. The mouth is slightly open.

This behaviour has to do with the sense of smell. Cats have something called Jacobson's organ located in two sacs lying just above the roof of their mouths. Normally, cats do not use this extra smelling organ. It is used mainly by entire cats during the mating game; for example, a male cat may smell a female cat by phleming to find out whether she is receptive or not. However, it can also be seen in neutered cats, most commonly when they are confronted by an unfamiliar smell or by a smell of urine in an odd place, such as outside a litter tray. When the cat raises its top lips, the two ducts open, so the cat can make use of Jacobson's organ.

BRINGING ITS OWNER DEAD ANIMALS

Most outdoor cats will sometimes present their owners with gifts of dead creatures, such as mice and birds, that they have caught. From the cat's point of view, this is perfectly natural, so it should not be punished, however unpleasant it may seem. Scolding the cat for bringing home prey will not stop it hunting; it will merely stop it from bringing it to its owner. As far as the cat is concerned, its owner is not a very good hunter, so needs to be taught a thing or two. A queen will bring home prey for her kittens to introduce them to hunting. For this reason, the behaviour is often seen in female cats, especially neutered ones that have no kittens of their own, but it is also seen in males.

BURYING ITS FAECES

This is an act of submission. A subordinate cat will bury its faeces so as not to demonstrate its presence to more dominant cats. On the other hand, a dominant cat will leave its faeces uncovered. Most pet cats, especially those kept on their own, will bury their faeces by scratching in the litter tray. This has nothing to do with cleanliness; it is simply a sign that the cat feels that its owner is dominant. In multi-cat households, you will often find that one or two cats leave their faeces uncovered, whereas the rest cover them.

WAGGING ITS TAIL

This often occurs when the cat is angry, but it actually means that the cat is feeling indecisive; it wants to do two things at once but cannot make up its mind which action to take.

EATING GRASS

Cats occasionally eat grass or, if they have no access to grass, house plants or anything similar. This often occurs when the cat needs to clean out its stomach by vomiting, for instance if it has furballs (see Chapter 7: Health care). Most cats vomit soon after they have eaten grass. Some experts argue that cats also eat grass to obtain folic acid, something that the cat needs in minute quantities for its well-being but cannot obtain from meat.

TAKING FOOD OUT OF ITS BOWL

This also is very common, and again experts argue as to why pet cats take pieces of food out of their feeding bowls, preferring to eat them on the floor next to the bowl. One theory, which seems to me to make sense, is that the cat finds the pieces of food too large and puts them outside the bowl so that it will be easier to chew them into smaller pieces. The fact that a cat never seems to remove dry food from its bowl, only tinned food which comes in much bigger chunks, supports this theory. Another theory is that the cat's bowl is too small. If the whiskers touch the sides of the bowl the cat may find it uncomfortable to eat, so will take out the food.

MAD HALF-HOUR

This is something which we always refer to as 'sod time' in our house! The cat, or cats, will charge around at a great speed, jumping on and off furniture and playing with everything in sight, usually with a wild look on their faces and flattened ears. It seems to occur more frequently in young cats (under five years of age) than older cats, but can happen at any age. This behaviour is usually seen late at night, around midnight, and is simply a way for an indoor cat to get rid of excess energy that it would have burnt off during the day if it had needed to go out and hunt for food.

SCRATCHING FURNITURE

Almost all indoor cats do this, particularly if they have not been introduced to a scratching post at an early enough age. The cat is simply sharpening its claws by stripping off an old sheath of claw to reveal a new, sharp one underneath. It is also a means of exercising its claws and paws, and of scent-marking; there are scent glands under its front paws. In a multi-cat household it will be the most dominant cats that are seen to scratch furniture, even if a scratching post is present, the subordinates sticking to the scratching post. It can be difficult to overcome this

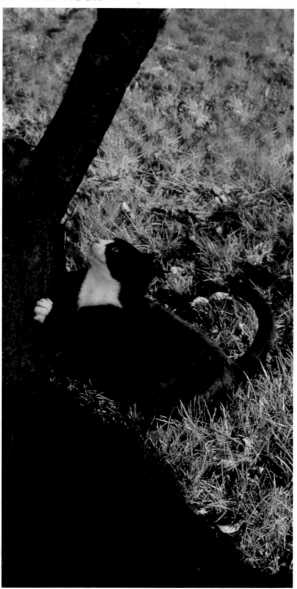

This cat is using a tree as a scratching post instead of its owner's furniture.   Photo: David Alderton

problem, and I have found that the best way is to buy furniture that is as cat resistant as possible. As mentioned earlier, if an interesting scratching post (preferably impregnated with catnip) is purchased at the same time as the kitten or cat, the like-lihood is that the cat will prefer this to any furniture. If not, one way of trying to dissuade the cat is to spray it from afar with a water pistol or spray bottle whenever the offending behaviour takes place. Shouting at the cat or punishing it in any other way has little or no effect. The advantage of the water pistol (and only ever use clean water) is that the jet hits the cat silently and unexpectedly; it will not suspect you as you will be a distance away.

SPRAYING

This habit, usually associated with sexual behaviour in unneutered male and female cats, can also be seen in male, and occasionally female, neuters. The spraying of urine is a normal and frequent act among entire males and cats that are allowed outside. It is a way of scent-marking the cat's territory. The cat will direct a small amount of urine, sometimes only a few drops, backwards against any vertical object, such as a tree or fence outdoors, or a cupboard or wall indoors. Spraying is always done when the cat is standing upright. The urine used is very concentrated and smells much stronger than ordinary urine. Unfortunately, as only a small amount is emitted, it can be very difficult to find a spray 'site' indoors; the smell is very evident but no wet patch can be found.

Normally a cat will have no need to spray indoors, as the house is the cat's accepted den, so no further enforcement is necessary. However, spraying may occur if the cat feels insecure or threatened in any way; for instance, because of the arrival of a new pet or a baby in the household or any other change in family circumstances, a house move or an increased challenge from a cat outdoors. Areas to be sprayed may include front doors and door mats if the owner's shoes have brought in alien smells, such as the scent of another, strange cat. Oriental breeds, especially Siamese, very often spray, and in these cases it may simply be because they feel frustrated or want more attention. The same behaviour can sometimes be seen in Siamese cross-breeds.

It is difficult to overcome the problem of spraying, but it can be done. Firstly, thor-oughly clean all the areas that have been sprayed, preferably with a disinfectant intended for the purpose, as many household detergents smell of ammonia, which will only attract the cat's attention. If an area smells of sprayed urine, it will often encourage the cat to use it again, or other cats to spray on top of it.

Secondly, place small amounts of dry cat food in each of these areas, as cats are reluctant to soil the place where they eat. If the food is eaten quickly and then spraying takes place afterwards, it may be worth trying to glue some pieces of dry food to a bowl, making it impossible for the cat to remove it.

If it is felt that the cat sprays because of an outside threat, such as the neighbour's vicious tom, boarding up any cat flaps in the house may be enough to reassure the cat that the house is its den and therefore secure.

Never punish a spraying cat; this only has the effect of increasing the cat's inse-curity. Cats that spray as a form of protest should be ignored except when their owners decide to give them attention; they should be cuddled, stroked and fed when the owner says so, and not receive any attention when they try to settle down on the owner's lap or ask for food. This reinforces the fact that the owner is dominant over the cat.

A bad sprayer can be confined to one room only, preferably a warm room where it can sleep next to a source of heat such as a radiator. The cat will probably feel secure in this room and so will not spray. If spraying ceases, the cat can be allowed access to the other rooms in the house one by one, under careful supervision. It is a good idea to put food down here and there to dissuade spraying.

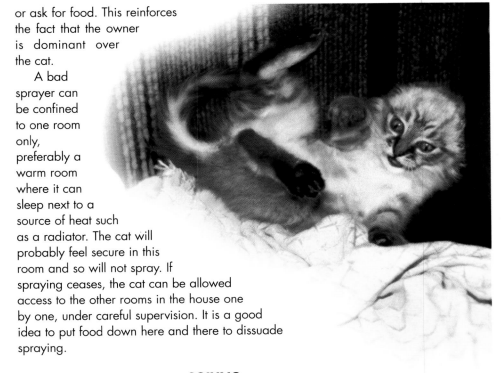

SOILING

Occasionally you may come across a cat that soils in places other than its litter tray. It will often do this where the smell of its owner is especially strong, such as on beds. It may occur when the owner is away on holiday and somebody else is looking after the cat in the owner's house.

There can be numerous reasons for cats soiling the house. Cats do not like to soil near to where they sleep or eat, so it may be just that the litter tray is wrongly positioned. Cats are very clean animals; they do not like to use dirty litter trays, so may go elsewhere if they feel the tray is dirty. Perhaps they do not like that particular brand of cat litter, so trying a different one may be worthwhile. Other cats want total privacy, and the litter tray may be placed in too public an area of the house. Always place the litter tray in a quiet corner and, if possible, use a hooded one.

Again, never punish a cat that soils outside its litter tray; this will only make the cat feel insecure and so make matters worse. Clean up any soiled areas thoroughly and place food in any such areas as you would for spraying. It may also be worth trying to prevent access to the favoured areas. Another good trick is to make the soiling areas unattractive to the cat by placing a plastic sheet over a bed that is being soiled, or some aluminium foil on an area on the floor. Cats do not like the feel of these under their feet. If all else fails, I have my own solution: put down rubber car mats in the places where soiling occurs. Then at least it's easier to clean up the mess!

chapter nine
marvellous moggies

This chapter is meant to highlight just how marvellous moggies can be. It contains a number of true life stories about non-pedigree cats, most of which have been through considerable hardship, only to find a new life in good, caring homes. Most of these cats have gone on to become top show-winning cats. All of the stories illustrate just how rewarding it can be to give a home to a rescued cat. Read them, and you will realise that there is no such thing as 'just a plain moggy'.

FELICIA

Felicia is one of the cats sharing a home with my husband Nick, our children Rebecca and Melanie, and me. Felicia is Rebecca's very own cat, one of a pair of tortoiseshell moggies. She is a tortie tabby with a small amount of white.

Felicia came to us one spring day in 1994 when Rebecca was only two years old. Heather, our friend and occasional child minder, telephoned and asked if she could bring over a kitten. She had rescued her from a friend, a lady with slight learning difficulties who suffered from sudden mood swings. Apparently the kitten had got in the way of one such mood swing. It was now limping badly, and had done so for some time. From what we later managed to gather, it seems likely that the poor kitten had been thrown against a wall in a fit of temper.

The kitten was approximately three months old and, apart from having one injured hind leg, also suffered from fleas and ear mites. On seeing it, little Rebecca happily exclaimed, 'Felix! Felix!' Felix was my very first cat, a non-pedigree

Facing page: Felicia, photographed by Alan Robinson.

tabby. When I left home, I decided to let Felix stay behind with my mother, as he was happy there. He still lives there today, aged 17, and Rebecca has met him on her visits to Sweden. She must have thought that this kitten looked just like him, despite the fact that it was a fraction of the size and a slightly different colour.

I sat down with the kitten on my lap, and she immediately settled, purring and being very friendly. Heather was surprised as, not surprisingly, the kitten previously had been a very nervous little cat. I examined the kitten and could clearly feel that her left hip was swollen, although I could not tell whether it was broken or not.

We all discussed what action to take. It was clear that the kitten needed a good home and veterinary care. However, we already had a houseful of cats and could certainly do without another one. We didn't know what sort of veterinary care the kitten was going to need but, quite apart from treatment for her injured hip, she would need vaccinations, blood tests for infectious diseases, and neutering. At that time we could not afford all those extra expenses, although we were very reluctant to hand the kitten over to a general animal shelter, as we would then never know what had become of her. She was in pain and, reluctantly, we came to the conclusion that it was best to save her from further suffering by having her

Hamish, probably a Siamese/Birman cross.

put to sleep. Luckily, Rebecca took such a liking to her that this never happened and now I find it hard to believe that we ever contemplated such a thing.

The following day we took the kitten to the vet, only to be told she would require X-rays to find out exactly what was wrong with her hip, and that any treatment was likely to be extensive. The vet was not prepared to give us more credit. He seemed to think us irresponsible to have taken on this kitten. We arrived back home in despair, with an untreated kitten.

Fortunately, help was not far away. We got in touch with the Yorkshire-based West Riding Pet Cat Club, of which we were members. We explained our predicament, as well as the fact that we were quite willing to give her a home. The WRPCC immediately agreed to take Felicia in and have her treated in any way that was necessary. After she had recovered she would be re-homed officially with us. This is but one example of the truly marvellous work done by this club.

Felicia stayed for a month with the chairman of the West Riding Pet Cat Club, Dawn Teague, and her family. The first thing was to assess the kitten's injuries. She was X-rayed and found to have a hip that was literally smashed to pieces. Furthermore, the injury had happened about three weeks earlier, so Felicia had been in pain for quite some time. Before surgery was attempted, she was blood-tested for the presence of Feline Leukaemia and Feline Immunodeficiency Virus, and happily was negative for both. She was then operated on, and her left hip joint had to be removed as it was too damaged to be repaired. Apparently this is not too uncommon an operation in cats and the muscles in the hip soon start to compensate for the lack of the joint. Felicia was ordered strict cage rest for a few weeks after her operation, then returned to us.

These days, anyone would be hard pushed to be able to tell that anything has ever been wrong with Felicia. She is like any other cat, full of life, running around playing with the other cats and with Rebecca. The only time it is noticeable that she has more or less lost part of one leg is in the evenings. After a day's play, Felicia's left hind leg gets rather tired, and then she will stop using it for a while. However, she is in no pain.

When Felicia was eight months old, we took her to her first cat show - entered in Rebecca's name, of course! She behaved impeccably all day, and was much admired by visitors, exhibitors and judges alike. In fact, one of the judges was a vet and, when told afterwards about Felicia's injury, she said she had never been able to guess.

Felicia swept the board at that very first show, winning her Whiskas class and also being made best overall Whiskas winner of that day, thus qualifying for the Supreme cat show and the prestigious Whiskas finals.

In her first 10 months as a show cat Felicia was entered in six shows. She proved to be a remarkably consistent winner, always gaining admiring glances. She was placed 38 times, with no less than 21 first prizes. Twice she was made Best In Show Household Pet, and she has won 11 trophies and many other awards. We are all very proud of her and her achievements but none more so than Rebecca and the West Riding Pet Cat Club. If it hadn't been for them, Felicia would not be alive today!

SOOTY

Sooty, a black-and-white non-pedigree owned by Miss Jill Hurn of Peterborough, was probably Britain's best known non-pedigree show cat. He was shown for 12 years and entered into a total of 844 classes, with first, second or third placings in 592 of them. Not many cats could beat that!

Sooty was born on the 9 September 1980. He was one of four kittens born to an ordinary tabby female. His father was the largest black tomcat in the village; it was a typical unplanned litter of kittens. He was Jill Hurn's very first cat. She had wanted a pet for company, but was out at work all day, so felt that a dog would not be suitable. Instead, she decided to get a cat and, when she went along to see the litter of kittens, Sooty promptly chose **her** rather than the other way round.

Sooty grew up into a very big, handsome cat: black, with white feet, white whiskers and a large white bib. People kept telling Jill that he was such a handsome cat that she ought to show him, so eventually she brought him along to the East of England Show in July 1982. Sooty was awarded no less than four first prizes, and was also Best in

Sooty, consistent show–winner up to the age of 14, with owner Jill Hurn.

Show of the household pets. Needless to say, his considerable success at his very first show spurred Jill on, and she continued to show him regularly. He always did well and all his judges' critiques praised his laid-back temperament and remarked how big he was. Sooty was soon labelled 'the perfect gentleman'.

Sooty competed at the Supreme Cat Show no less than 11 times. In 1990, at the age of 10, he received the ultimate accolade: he was voted Best in Show Household Pet. As if this wasn't enough, he was also runner-up to the Best Whiskas Cat at the Supreme that year. He had previously been a runner-up in the Whiskas finals at the 1986 Supreme, and become Whiskas Cat of the Year in 1988 by beating all the other Whiskas finalists. During all his years at the Supreme Sooty was unplaced only twice.

Apart from the successes at the Supreme show, Sooty and Jill enjoyed considerable success at other shows all over the country. No less than nine times was Sooty made Best in Show in the Household Pet Section.

Shows were not everything in Sooty's life. At home he loved to sit on Jill's knee, his other favourite spots including the airing cupboard and the back bedroom bed, which caught a great deal of sun. Sooty would walk on a lead outdoors, and he often used to accompany Jill on visits to her elderly aunt. When the aunt moved into a care home, Sooty accompanied Jill on visits, bringing much pleasure to the other residents as well. Sooty also accompanied Jill to choir practice and to the Women's Institute. He was a marvellous traveller and was never bothered at all by all his journeys to shows.

Sooty died on 4 August 1994, just a month after his final show. He suffered a stroke and peacefully slipped away. It was the end of a long and very happy life.

TABBIA

Mrs Iris Burgess, a breeder of pedigree cats, had a successful non-pedigree show cat who had had a very unusual start in life. Tabbia and her brother were born in the middle of a lawn to a feral cat. The lady who owned the lawn watched the birth from her kitchen window. A couple of hours later their mother disappeared, leaving the tiny newborns all on their own, totally exposed. Realising that their mother was not going to come back, the lady carefully put the two kittens in a lined box and contacted the local vet who suggested she contacted Mrs Burgess, whose Manx cat, Nina, was due to have a litter of kittens any day. Nina had already developed milk, so was given the two orphan kittens to care for. The kittens immediately started to suckle their foster mother. Nina cared for them well, and duly gave birth to her own litter two days later. Eventually a home was found for the male kitten, who was a semi-longhaired ginger-and-white. The female kitten stayed with Mrs Burgess and was named Tabbia. She was a pretty and unusual silver tabby tortoiseshell.

Rather appropriately, Tabbia's first show was the Tabby Club show. She loved being at the show, taking it all in her stride, like so many non-pedigree cats. She gained two firsts, a third and a fifth and was nominated for Best in Show. She did not win BIS on this occasion but was a worthy runner-up. Tabbia has been to more shows, always being very well placed. Indeed, she won Best Overall Whiskas at her very first attempt.

Sadly, Mrs Burgess was taken ill at the end of 1994 and was forced to re-home some of her cats, including Tabbia. But Tabbia now enjoys life to the full with a pleasant family who well and truly spoil her.

PANSY

Pansy is my daughter Rebecca's other cat. Pansy became Rebecca's very own cat as a young kitten, when Rebecca herself was only six months old. As with Rebecca's other cat, Felicia, it was very much a case of kitten and child choosing one another. Appropriately, Pansy and Felicia are also inseparable, one of them hardly ever to be seen without the other.

Pansy is a very pretty tortoiseshell-and-white moggy. Her official name for shows is 'Patchwork Pansy' as it describes her looks so well.

Pansy came to us from a pet shop, just like our tabby-and-white Benji, who was mentioned in an earlier chapter. My husband, Nick, went to a pet shop in a town nearby to deliver some hamsters we had bred. On arriving back home he handed me a large cardboard box. When I opened it I found little Pansy inside. Apparently, it had been the all-too-common story of kittens in pet shops. Pansy was flea-ridden and very small, and Nick had taken pity on her. She was said to have been eight weeks old at the time, but we sincerely doubted this. At that time we had a litter of Persian kittens that were exactly eight weeks old and, even allowing for their long coats, they appeared absolutely enormous next to little Pansy. We estimated that she was no more than six weeks at the most and she certainly was not fully weaned. However, despite fleas and worms, she was a healthy little cat, and settled in very quickly with our other cats. Once Rebecca started to talk, one of her first ever words was 'baby', and for a while we could not quite work out why she kept saying this, over and over again. Then we realised that she was referring to Pansy. Pansy has been her little baby ever since and, together with Felicia, is often seen fast asleep in Rebecca's dolls' pram.

We started showing Pansy as a kitten and she has had considerable success. At her very first show she was nominated for Best in Show, although she did not win the award. She has qualified for the Supreme Cat Show more times than we can remember

Gizmo, one of Britain's top-winning non-pedigree cats.
Photo: Marc Henrie

Felicia winning BIS Household Pet, with judge Janice Ackerman from the USA.

and has an impressive array of trophies. The first time we showed her at the Supreme, we decorated her pen along the lines of Rebecca's pet name for her: Baby. Pansy's pen was therefore turned into a cot, complete with bedding, bumper and mobile, and she had such a comfortable time that she would rather have stayed in her pen all day.

GIZMO

Gizmo is probably one of Britain's most successful non-pedigree show cats in recent years, although he has only been shown for a short time. This very distinctive semi-longhaired white-and-black cat with a black nose is owned by Miss Pamela Wells of Chippenham, Wiltshire.

The Wells family used to live in Dunfermline, Scotland, and it was there that Gizmo turned up as a stray kitten in their back garden in December 1990. He was approximately four months old. The Wells family did all they could to find his rightful owner but, despite all their efforts, nobody came forward. To start with, the family said that the kitten would definitely not be staying with them; they would just look after it until its owner was found. Needless to say, Gizmo had soon settled in and was there to stay.

In January 1992 Pamela went along to a local cat show as a spectator. She was delighted to find that non-pedigrees could be shown. Soon Gizmo was entered for his first show, the Nor'east of Scotland Cat Club show in Dundee. Describing the day in her own words, Pamela says: 'I was so worried that Gizmo would get upset and hate showing, but the only one to cry that day was myself. Gizmo was entered in seven classes that day. He won five firsts and two seconds, and also his first Best in Show.'

Pamela went on showing Gizmo over the next few months, and had considerable success, including two more Best in Show wins, and a second placing at his first visit to the Supreme. The following year saw several more Best in Show wins. Gizmo also acquired a new friend. Pamela rescued two feral kittens from a farm and kept one of them, whom she called Hercules. Hercules soon joined Gizmo on the show bench and won Best in Show at his very first outing! Both cats qualified for the Whiskas finals at the Supreme in 1993, and both cats won their classes and their groups. Neither of them went any further, but that day was a very successful one.

During 1994 Gizmo wasn't shown quite as much as earlier, but he made it to the Supreme, and this time he was actually made Whiskas Pet of the Year. As Pamela says, 'I was so delighted I still smile when I think about it.' Pamela has four cats in all, and even several months later they had not managed to eat all the food that Gizmo had won for them. Pamela, big-hearted as usual, donated some of it to a local rescue centre. During 1995, Gizmo was injured so did not get to many shows. However, he managed to qualify for the Supreme, where he was made Best HP Longhair In Show.

Gizmo's latest triumph is to become Supreme Non-Pedigree Exhibit 1996 at the Supreme Cat Show. Well done, Gizmo!

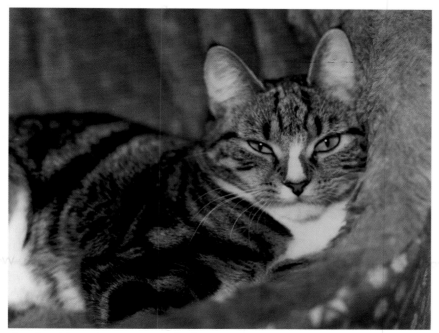

Comfortable and cosy in a cat bed.

HAMISH

The story of Hamish does not have a happy ending, but I felt that it should be included here to illustrate just what some non-pedigree cats have to go through simply because they are seen as 'worthless' by far too many people. Hamish belonged to my husband and me, and to us he was anything but worthless; he was a much-loved member of our family.

Hamish was born to two pedigree parents of different breeds in 1989. We will never really know for certain what his breeding was, but it was said to have been one Siamese and one Persian. Certainly, Hamish was half Siamese, but to have gained his long fur, his tabby-pointed face with brilliant blue eyes, and other features not common to ordinary Persians, he was more likely to have had one Birman parent. Hamish was the runt of the litter, born somewhere in Scotland a few days after his litter-mates. When he was only two weeks old, his 'breeder' (although I would not wish to call this person a breeder) felt that he was unlikely to survive and sold him for one pound to a lorry driver from Doncaster, Yorkshire, where we live. How the kitten managed to survive at such a tender age is beyond all understanding but, at around four weeks of age, Hamish was wandering the streets of Doncaster, being used as a small child's plaything. The lorry driver had given the kitten to his sister, and their younger brother was soon seen to chase the kitten around. Nick and I first spotted the scruffy looking kitten in our front garden, being chased by the little boy and our neighbour's children. When we enquired about the kitten, our neighbour told us that he belonged to the older sister of the little boy, but that he would probably soon be homeless. The girl was meant to be moving to a flat where no pets were allowed and her mother, who was allergic to cats, would not be able to keep the kitten. Later that day, when the kitten still had not been collected by its owner, our neighbour handed him to us, feeling that it would be better if we took care of him. Nick found out where the kitten's owners lived and went to ask if we could keep the kitten. The mother of the family was more than willing to let us have the cat, as it would soon have nowhere to live anyway. The kitten's actual owner, her daughter, had just gone on holiday, and the mother was none too pleased about having been left with the kitten.

So the kitten stayed with us. He was a sorry sight. On examining the little male we found him to be full of fleas and ear mites. His fur was badly matted and very dirty. His stomach was so distended with worms that there was room for hardly any food, and the poor little cat was so weak that he displayed no normal kitten characteristics (such as playing) at all. In fact, he was hardly able to walk. We groomed him, bathed him and fed him, and after that he fell fast asleep.

The following day we brought him to our vet. The vet, who was Scottish, suggested we name him Hamish. He confirmed that Hamish could not be much more than four weeks old. The vet felt so sorry for him that he waived his fee, and we went home with ear drops and worming pills and started to bring Hamish back to health.

Hamish recovered and grew up quickly. One of his special friends was our Siamese, no doubt because he somehow knew that he was part-Siamese. His other special friend was our Cocker Spaniel bitch Bonnie, who regularly suffered from phantom pregnancies. Bonnie adopted little Hamish as her 'puppy' and cared for him, protected him and even disciplined him as she felt fit.

We soon realised that Hamish was not a very clever cat; in fact we soon started referring to him, affectionately of course, as 'the clod'. Hamish never behaved quite like other cats. He was clumsy, very clumsy, and would regularly fall off chairs and tables or down the stairs. Unlike other cats, he never landed on all four feet; he usually landed on his head. He even fell out of an upstairs window once, landing on his head. No matter how many times he fell, it never seemed to bother him, and he never seemed to be hurt. We learnt to take special care with Hamish. Whereas you could happily pick any of the other cats up from, say, the dinner table, and drop it onto the floor, this could never be done with Hamish. He would even fall off his resting place on the cat scratching post when he fell asleep. Apart from falling often, Hamish also had an incredible knack for knocking things over; more like a bull in a china shop than a graceful cat! Still, we never bothered too much about any of this, and loved Hamish as he was.

Among Hamish's other peculiarities was sudden memory loss. If, for instance, he was in the kitchen with another cat, and the other cat left, Hamish would sometimes forget where the door was, and would wander around the kitchen wailing, pleading for somebody to find him. On other, more distressing, occasions he would forget who a family member was and run away frightened when approached by somebody in whom he had previously had great trust. The same went for the other cats, especially if one of them had been away for a short while, like a queen going away for mating. On its arrival back home, Hamish would have forgotten who the cat was and would, for a few days, treat it as a total stranger. On the other hand, he absolutely adored kittens, being very kitten-like himself, and always warmly welcomed any new member of the household.

We used to say that Hamish had but two moods: his floppy mood and his stick mood. When he was relaxed, he was thoroughly relaxed, and went floppy like a ragdoll when handled, purring happily. When he was nervous, he would go stiff as a stick, with eyes large and round. Sometimes we considered the possibility that he was slightly brain-damaged but, as he was happy and healthy, we never explored this. We felt we were all happier not knowing.

When Hamish was about a year old we took him to a local pet show, just to show him off to people. We penned him in a large rabbit show pen, and this was when we discovered that he loved being kept in a pen. He would purr and rub up against anybody who touched him. Presumably he felt secure inside a pen. Remembering this, we entered Hamish for the non-pedigree section at our local championship cat show later that year. Once again Hamish loved being in the pen, and he so impressed the judges with his friendliness that he won eight awards in all, including a first in his Whiskas class, which qualified him for the open class at the Supreme show the following year. Hamish would go stiff and start to worry as soon as he was outside his pen, but inside it he was as happy as could be. We continued to show him, and his second show was none other than the Supreme. The judge there commented on how laid back and relaxed he was, and Hamish won his class. From then on, we continued to take Hamish to shows, and he never went home without any awards. In fact, it was really Hamish who started off our interest in showing.

The years went past and, when Hamish was five, his behaviour became more peculiar than ever, and in a very distressing way. He started attacking our other cats, his former friends, viciously and seriously. The attacks would come totally out of the blue and, afterwards, Hamish would seem to have forgotten that they had ever taken place. He would be very upset when the cat he had attacked just a few minutes earlier would refuse to come near him out of fear and anger. The attacks became more and more frequent, involving more and more of the cats. One day Hamish savagely attacked his best friend, Tolly, the Siamese. I found Tolly, normally a very forward and bold cat, huddling in a corner, covered in blood and excrement, where he had messed himself out of fear. The poor thing had no idea why he had been attacked and Hamish, of course, had forgotten that he had done it. Tolly still wanted to be friends with Hamish but gradually grew more and more frightened of him. We took Hamish to the vet, looking for an answer to this sudden, weird behaviour. We told Hamish's life story as we knew it and he was examined thoroughly. The vet came to the conclusion that Hamish was brain-damaged, no doubt because he had not been properly reared as a young kitten. He had a Taurine deficiency, the most common result of which is blindness, but which can also cause brain damage. Hamish was now slowly going blind and he clearly had some brain disorder. We were given various pills to try to calm him down, but to no avail. Hamish continued the attacks on our other cats, and they became more and more frequent, eventually involving three different cats in one day. The vet said he would get worse and might eventually start to attack people as well.

After a while things had gone so far that we had to keep Hamish totally separated from the other cats. On his own, he was the same loving cat, but he was also desperately unhappy without feline company. It was clear that things could not go on as they were. Re-homing was not an option, as he could never again be trusted with other cats, although he was not happy without them, and he was very wary of strangers except at the shows. Reluctantly, we took the only decision that was left to us: we had Hamish put to sleep.

Hamish died in my arms after several injections at the vet's. As usual, he did not react like an ordinary cat, not even to the lethal injection. He needed a much bigger dose than any other cat. He didn't suffer, however, and eventually just slipped away. We will all miss him forever, and we will never forget our so-special cat, whose downfall was simply that he had not been cared for as a kitten.

Tolly, despite having been attacked so viciously by his friend, missed Hamish so desperately that, after more than two months, we had to buy another Siamese as a companion for him. Luckily, these days Tolly is very happy with his new companion and seems to have forgotten about Hamish altogether.

HEBE AND ARNIE

Hebe and Arnie are two very special cats who can only be described as 'stars'. Both are owned by Mrs Dawn Teague, the chairman of the West Riding Pet Cat Club.

Hebe is a ginger female who was brought into the WRPCC's welfare section with her mother and three litter-mates. At the tender age of six weeks Hebe was in the television series *Heartbeat* starring Nick Berry. She played the part of a kitten that was found inside a sack in a river, having been left to die. The episode was screened in November 1993, and over 15 million people watched the little kitten being rescued, and eventually given a home with the series police sergeant, Blaketon. A year later, Hebe returned for an episode of *Heartbeat* and this time was seen by 18 million viewers. But between these two episodes Hebe had had a bad accident. At the age of four months, she managed to fall behind the Teague family's cooker, ending up with her lower jaw fractured in three places. Even the vet doubted that she would survive, but she pulled through and has starred in other television programmes since then.

Hebe's companion Arnie is a black male (neuter) cat. He was re-homed through the WRPCC welfare section, only to be returned later by his new owners, who claimed that he was biting. Despite this it wasn't long before Arnie starred in an episode of *Heartbeat*, behaving so impeccably that the director of the programme even decided that she wanted more scenes starring Arnie than had originally been planned. Arnie played the pet of an old woman believed by children to be a witch, and had to be handled by a child, as well as sitting on the knee of the old lady. He also had several scenes where he had to perform certain tasks to order, such as running through a door. Arnie behaved like the star he is, and nobody would have believed that this cat had been accused of being unreliable.

Hebe, feline star of *Heartbeat*, with human star Nick Berry and owner Dawn Teague.

Dilys Marvin with her successful ginger show cat, Leo.

LEO

Leo is just one of many cats owned by Dilys Marvin, a very well-known lady in non-pedigree show circles. Dilys runs the Cat's Whiskers boarding cattery, as well as the Catwatch charity which re-homes many unwanted and abandoned cats. Catwatch is to be seen at most major GCCF shows, where Dilys sells items such as key-rings and notepaper to raise money for her rescue work.

Leo is a large ginger neuter male. He was found on a rubbish tip in August 1985 with his mother and three other kittens. The mother cat was in such poor condition, including dehydration, that she could no longer care for her kittens, so Dilys had to hand-rear them. The mother eventually recovered and she and three of the four kittens were successfully re-homed. Leo, however, stayed with Dilys at Catwatch.

Leo is a striking cat, very well known at shows. He has gained many awards, including Best in Show Household Pet two years in a row at the Bedford show (1991 and 1992), BIS Household Pet, again two years in a row, at the Yorkshire County Cat Club show (1992 and 1993), and he has been an overall Whiskas heat winner no less than four times. To top it all, he was Runner-up Non-Pedigree Exhibit and the best shorthaired at the 1996 Supreme Cat Show.

TIPPI

Tippi was another hand–reared cat, the very first rescued moggy that my husband, Nick, and I took on. A friend of ours, Tilly, was walking her dogs in the woods near her home in Kent one day in 1988 when one of them spotted a cardboard box. The bitch showed such an interest that Tilly went to examine it and, upon doing so, found five tiny kittens no more than 10 days old. Doubtless, the kittens had been dumped by an uncaring owner who did not want them and hoped they would die. How anybody can be so cruel as to leave kittens to starve, not to mention taking an entire litter of kittens from a queen, is just beyond comprehension.

Tilly brought the kittens home and hand-reared them all - not an easy task, as each kitten had to be fed at two-hourly intervals, day and night. Nick and I first saw the kittens when they were two to three weeks old, and it wasn't long before Nick had promised Tilly that we would give a home to one of them.

When the kittens were six

Tippi

weeks old and could feed themselves, little Tippi came to live with us. She was a tabby-and-white female. Never really having had any contact with cats other than her litter-mates she did not quite know how to behave. To start with, she couldn't even miaow. Our only other cat at that time was Blondie, a female Persian then five months old. Blondie, having been an only cat and a very spoilt one at that, immediately detested little Tippi. She would hiss and growl at the tiny kitten, and was not above giving her a smack in the face if she felt it necessary. However, Tippi, not knowing any better, just assumed that this was normal feline behaviour and copied Blondie in everything that she did, including returning the smacks. Blondie, who was nearly four times as big as Tippi, could not understand how Tippi could be so cheeky: Tippi, who was so small that her bed was a box of tissues!

For a while we doubted that Blondie and Tippi ever would become firm friends, but one day something happened that altogether changed Blondie's attitude. Nick and I kept two pet rats indoors, and their cage was located on a coffee table in the studio flat where we then lived. The rats did not like the cats as they had previously been scratched by Blondie through the bars of their cage. This particular day, I was in the bathroom hanging the washing when I suddenly heard a terrible scream coming from the other room. It was obviously Tippi, and for a moment I was convinced that Blondie had finally had enough of her and decided to kill her. I dropped everything and rushed out to rescue Tippi.

The sight that met me was not quite what I had expected. Tippi was sitting on the coffee table, next to the rats' cage. One of her ears was stuck inside the cage, having been pulled through the bars by one of the rats, which now had a firm grip on it with its teeth. Tippi pulled in one direction, the rat in another, and the poor kitten must have been in terrible pain. Meanwhile, Blondie was running backwards and forwards, looking terribly worried. If she had been able to talk, I'm sure that she would have been shouting, 'It wasn't me, it wasn't me!' over and over again.

I managed to free Tippi and luckily the damage to her ear was not too bad, although she did have a small scar for the rest of her life. Whilst I was cleaning Tippi's wound, Blondie came over. She looked very concerned, and suddenly started to wash Tippi, wanting to care for her. Tippi didn't mind this at all and, from that day onwards, the two cats were best of friends.

A few months later we moved to our house in Yorkshire and Tippi soon became a very typical cat. Gone were the days when she didn't know how cats behaved; now she was an outdoor cat who regularly brought in mice. One thing that stayed with her forever, though, was her love of dolls' milk bottles. Having been hand-reared by Tilly, she never quite forgot that experience. One day I was hand-rearing some rat kittens when Tippi suddenly spotted the bottle and grabbed it. She still remembered how to drink from it and, from that day on, drinking from a doll's bottle became her party piece, showed off to many friends. Tippi would lay on her back on anybody's lap and hold the bottle with her paws, gently squeezing it to receive the milk.

Sadly, Tippi died at the age of just six years. One night she was attacked viciously by a dog specially trained to kill cats and, despite an extensive operation and several weeks of treatment, she never recovered, and had to be put to sleep because she was suffering. She had one last bottle before she went to sleep forever, although Nick had to hold it for her as her paws were too weak. She may have been our first rescued moggy, but she will certainly not be our last.

BARNABY

Master Barnaby is a longhaired cream cat, born 15 June 1984. His owner, Ann Mott from Bury St Edmunds, also owned his mother, a red Tabby named Mrs Tiggy Winkle, whom she acquired as a kitten from a local farm. Barnaby's father is described as a 'half-pedigree black Persian'.

There were four kittens in the litter, but Barnaby won his owners' hearts. As the kittens approached 12 weeks of age, Ann's husband would enquire whether a new home had been found for Barnaby, as by this time new homes had been found for all his siblings. Silence was the only answer he ever received.

Ann took Barnaby to his first cat show, staged as part of an agricultural show, when he reached 12 weeks of age. When the judging started all the owners were asked to leave the tent for a few hours, so Ann and her husband went off to enjoy the rest of the show. When they returned, they found a hoard of people crowded around Barnaby's pen. The little kitten had won everything, including BIS! After this, Ann's husband never asked when Barnaby would be re-homed.

In the following years, Barnaby had a meteoric show career, with numerous awards, including Third Runner-up at the Supreme Cat Show. Then tragedy struck. In 1990, on the day of Ann's son's wedding, the family received a telephone call from friends who were looking after Ann's house to say that Barnaby had been hit by a car and left for dead in the road. They called an emergency vet, who attended Barnaby at home. Meanwhile, Ann and her husband drove the 10 miles home to be with their beloved 'boy'.

Barnaby was in a bad way, his jaw badly torn and fractured, but the vet's verdict was that he stood a good chance of survival since he was such a big cat, weighing a hefty 7.7kg (16lb). Ann and her husband slept downstairs with him that night to keep an eye on him and make sure he kept warm enough. In fact, his recovery began that very night.

He managed to get up and find a warmer spot and, by morning, had even managed to use the litter tray. Remarkably, he had not even attempted to remove the bandages that bound his jaw.

The following day entailed a further visit to the vet who, although it was Sunday, stitched and wired Barnaby's jaw. Typically, Barnaby wasn't having any of the soft-soap approach; he turned his nose up at the soft foods the vet had advised for him and started eating biscuits instead!

Within three weeks, brave Barnaby was back to full health and fit to attend his next show, only having missed one since his accident. However, his accident had put him off shows in some way; he now disliked being handled by strangers. For this reason, Ann retired him from the show circuit.

To this day, Barnaby lives happily with Ann's pedigree cats, adores their kittens and generally enjoys life. Since the accident, he has never been allowed out - and has shown no desire to go. Barnaby is, Ann says, a very happy and contented pet cat.

A marvellous moggy!

index